Self-help to
English Conversation

Published by
Lotus Press Publishers & Distributors

Self-help to English Conversation

Jim Peterson

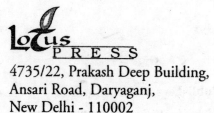

4735/22, Prakash Deep Building,
Ansari Road, Daryaganj,
New Delhi - 110002

Lotus Press Publishers & Distributors
Unit No.220, 2nd Floor, 4735/22, Prakash Deep Building,
Ansari Road, Daryaganj, New Delhi- 110002
Ph:- 32903912, 23280047, 098118-38000
Email : lotuspress1984@gmail.com
Visit us : www.lotuspress.co.in

Self-help to English Conversation
© 2016, Jim Peterson
ISBN : 81-8382-133-2

All rights reserved. No part of this publication may be reproduced,
stored in a retrieval system, or transmitted, in any form or by any
means, mechanical, photocopying, recording or otherwise, without
prior written permission of the publisher.

Printed & Published by : **Lotus Press Publishers & Distributors,** New Delhi- 2

PREFACE

Conversation is a basic human need that leads to normal working of everyday life. Over the past few centuries, English has grown to be a common language of interaction between people of different nationalities. Its significance and influence in the present day world can be seen in the fact that is being increasingly chosen as a medium of communication in schools, colleges, offices and even in public places. This stands as a foremost reason why many people who cannot converse well in English feel inferior when they find themselves in a situation where they are required to choose the language as a medium of communication.

At the same time when it is important to be able to speak fluently in English, it is also imperative that one speaks in a manner that leaves a lasting impression on the listener. Such a conversation involves a blend of tactful choice of words and an impressive way of speaking. The speaker should be well aware of the grammar of the language and various phrases, idioms, jargons and lingos, etc. in use. When using phrases and jargons, one should be sensitive towards the listeners with whom he is speaking. At the same time, the mood of the conversation should also be considered.

The present book 'Self-help to English Conversation' leads the readers onto the road of picking tips and strategies for conversing effectively in English language. Apart from stressing on grammar needed for speaking correctly, the book also elaborates on different idioms commonly used in conversation and how to help children with special needs to converse properly.

Author

CONTENTS

Other Books on

WORD POWER SERIES

CHAPTER 1

Conversation is an Art

Several epochs in modern history have been productive of brilliant conversationalists. In Shakespeare's time, for example, we know that congenial spirits found greatest pleasure in conversing, and it may be taken for granted that a keen wit and ready response characterised the sparkling flow of language.

Speaking is a skill that you cannot acquire on your own, as you need someone to talk to. The more you talk to others, the more skilled you are in spealking fluently. So, in order to be a good speaker, one must not miss an opportunity to talk to others. If you are a housewife, talk to your family members and neighbours. If you are a student, you may talk to your classmates, teachers and friends.

If you are an employee, you may talk to your colleagues and so on. Try to speak as much as possible, without getting worried about the mistakes you make. Remember that no one is perfect!

Above all, be confident. Don't be afraid to speak. One must try to speak, even if you make mistakes. You cannot learn without making mistakes. There is a saying, "The person who never made a mistake never made anything." So think of your mistakes as something positive and useful. As already mentioned, speak as much as possible. Make as many mistakes as possible. That is the right way to learn and gain perfection.

Also, be positive and optimistic. Do not treat the mistakes you make as failures. Rather, when you know that you have made a mistake, you know that you have made progress.

However, as far as speaking in public is concerned, there should be a good preparation, as with a good preparation and planning, you will feel confident. And, your audience will feel your confidence. This way, your audience, too, will be confident. They will be confident in you. And, this will give you control of your audience and of your presentation. With control, you will be 'in charge' and your audience will listen positively to what you speak.

There are no physical conditions necessary for becoming a good orator. Even a man having painful obstruction in his speech can be far more agreeable than all the fluent people in the room. When a man comes to consider by what conditions conversation can be improved, and turns first of all to his own side to see what he can do for himself in that direction, he will find that certain natural gifts which he may possess, or the absence of which he may regret, are of no small importance in making him more agreeable to those whom he meets in society. It seems desirable to mention these at the outset for completeness' sake, and also that educators may lay their foundations in children for after use in the world.

Always Remember

"To talk well and eloquently is a very great art, but that an equally great one is to know the right moment to stop."

– Wolfgang Amadeus Mozart

Tips and Strategies

Talk often, but never long; in that case, if you do not please, at least you are sure not to tire your hearers. Pay your own reckoning, but do not treat the whole company–this being one of the very few cases in which people do not care to be treated, every one being fully convinced that he has means to pay.

Never hold anybody by the button or the hand in order to be heard out; for if people are not willing to hear you, you had much better hold on your tongue than them. Most long talkers single out some unfortunate man in company whom they observe to be the most silent, or their next neighbour to whisper, or at least in a half voice to convey a continuity of words to. This is excessively ill bred, and in some degree a fraud–conversation stock being a joint and common property. But on the other hand, if one of the unmerciful talkers lays hold of you, hear him with patience, and at least seeming attention, if he is worth obliging for nothing will oblige him more than a patient hearing, as nothing would hurt him more than either to leave him in the midst of his discourse, or to discover your impatience under your affliction.

Avoid as much as you can, in mixed companies, argumentative, political conversations–which though they should not, yet certainly do, indispose for a time the contending parties toward each other; and if the controversy grows warm and noisy, make an effort to put an end to it by some genteel levity or joke.

You may sometimes hear some people in good company interlard their discourse with oaths, by way of embellishment, as they think; but you must observe, too, that those who do so are never those who contribute in any degree to give that company the denomination of good company. They are always subalterns, or people of low education; for that practice, besides that it has no one temptation to plead, is as silly and illiberal as it is wicked.

Some people abruptly speak advantageously of themselves, without either pretence or provocation. They are impudent. Others proceed more artfully as they imagine, and forge accusations against themselves, complain of calumny which they never heard, in order to justify themselves by exhibiting a catalogue of their many virtues. However, above all things, and upon all occasions, avoid speaking of yourself, if it be possible. Such is the natural pride and vanity of our hearts that it perpetually breaks out, even in people of the best parts, in all the various modes and figures of the egotism.

It is often advisable to adapt your conversation to the people you are conversing with. A man of the world must, like the chameleon, be able to take every different hue, which is by no means criminal or abject, but a necessary complaisance; for it relates only to manners and not to morals.

CHAPTER 2

Skills to Converse

As most would agree, some people express themselves quite well, whereas others feel timid, hesitant and reluctant to talk or participate in a discussion. And, their lack of confidence is obvious to all. As conversation lessons and exercises are intended to improve conversational skills, it is necessary to first focus on building skills by eliminating some of the barriers that might prohibit the participants from participating in a discussion.

Fluency

Fluency is very important in speaking. However, if your conversation is full of grammatical errors, your ideas will not get across so easily.

Studying grammar rules will certainly help you speak more accurately.

Planning your Learning

The following is a recommended way to pursue your grammar learning for speaking systematically through self-access learning.

Step 1 - Identify the areas of deficiency in your speaking.

- Ask a friend or an elder who speaks correct and fluent English to analyse your speaking output to clarify the actual problem, e.g. vocabulary, sentence structure, tenses, lack of practice, etc.

- Establish with your friend what you need to focus on, like fluency or accuracy.

Step 2 - Prioritise the aspects of grammar you need to improve.

- You may find it easier to make and evaluate progress if you focus on one or two areas at a time rather than trying to improve everything at the same time.

- In self-access learning, you have the freedom to select and prioritise what aspects of grammar you feel you need to learn.

Step 3 - Set your learning goals and make a concrete self-access learning plan.

- Devise a short or long term plan by considering questions like 'What?', 'How?', 'When?', 'How long?', 'Plan Achieved?', etc. You can change your plan whenever necessary.

- Plan and stick to programmes of work where long-term learning is concerned, e.g. dealing with ingrained mistakes, etc.

Step 4 - Choose grammar exercises that meet with your needs and learning styles.

- Try out different materials to see which one suits you when you devise your self-access learning plan. You need exercises, which encourage you to check how the rules you have learned apply to actual English sentences in context.

Step 5 - Arrange a regular time to practise, and constantly review the progress and problems.

- Good language skills always need active and persistent practice. Learners are advised to arrange regular time to study. Some suggestions are:

- Join discussion groups for active practice to experiment and reinforce the learned rules.

- In order to evaluate your progress, whenever you work on a particular grammar point, try self-testing with the exercises and the answer key in the material before and after you study the grammar aspect.

- When you find it difficult to evaluate your own progress, seek help from your friends and elders to comment on your grammar in speaking.

CHAPTER 3

Grammar for Speaking

Grammar is a system of a language. Though it is described by many as the 'rules' of a language, but, as a matter of fact, no language has rules. If we use the word 'rules', we suggest that somebody created the rules first and then spoke the language. However, languages did not start like that. Languages began to exist when people started making sounds which evolved into words, phrases and sentences. No commonly spoken language is fixed. All languages change over time. What we call 'grammar' is simply a reflection of a language at a particular time.

However, if you are keen upon learning a foreign language, it is necessary to learn grammar, as it can help you to learn a language more quickly and more efficiently. It's important to think of grammar as something that can help you like a friend. Understanding the grammar (or system) of a language would enable you to understand many things yourself, without having to ask a teacher or look in a book.

So think of grammar as something good, something positive and something that you can use to find your way like a signpost or a map.

Parts of Speech

In English, speech is divided into different parts. Each part has a specific purpose to make the speech complete and comprehensible. Have a look at these parts.

Verbs

Verbs are sometimes described as 'action words'. Many verbs give the idea of action, of 'doing' something. For example, words like *run, fight, do* and *work,* all convey action.

However, it is only partly true. Some verbs do not give the idea of action; they give the idea of existence, of state, of 'being'. For example, verbs like *be, exist, seem* and *belong,* all convey states.

In simple terms, therefore, we can say that verbs are words that tell us what a subject *does* or *is*, they describe:

- *Action* (Tarun *walks* briskly.)
- *State* (The old woman *seems* honest.)

Terminology

Here are some of the terms used in discussing verbs and tenses.

Mood

Indicative mood expresses a simple statement of fact which can be positive (affirmative) or negative. A few examples are given below:

- I *enjoy* Indian classical music.
- I *do* not *enjoy* Indian classical music.

  Interrogative mood expresses a question

- Why *do* you *enjoy* Indian classical music?

  Imperative mood expresses a command

- *Sit down!*

  Subjunctive mood expresses what is imagined or wished or possible

- The commander ordered that the army *launch* attack.

Voice

Voice represents the relationship of the subject to the action. In the *active voice*, the subject does the action (*Megha picks* the ball). In the *passive voice*, the subject receives the action (The ball is *picked by Megha*). Among other things, we can use voice to help us change the focus of attention.

Aspect

Aspect expresses a feature of the action related to time, such as completion of the action or its duration. Present simple and past simple tenses have no aspect, but if we wish we can stress so with other tenses in the following manner:

- The action or state referred to by the verb is completed (and often still relevant), for example:

  I *have returned* the computer to Nitin. (So, now he do not have the computer.)

  (This is called *perfective aspect*, using perfect tenses.)

- The action or state referred to by the verb is in progress or continuing (that is, uncompleted), for example:

  We *are reading*.

  (This is called *progressive aspect*, using progressive [continuous] tense.)

Verb Classification

We can divide verbs into the following broad classifications:

Helping Verbs

Consider the following sentences:

- I *do*.
- People *must*.
- The student *will*.

These sentences do not make any meaning. That's because the verbs in the above sentences are *helping verbs* and have no meaning on their own. Helping verbs are usually used with main verbs. They 'help' the main verb. (The sentences in the above examples are, therefore, incomplete. They need at least a main verb to complete them.)

Primary helping verbs

These are the verbs *be*, *do* and *have*. These three verbs can be used as helping verbs or as main verbs. First, consider their use as helping verbs. They are used in the following cases:

- *Be*
  - To make continuous tenses (She *is* knitting a sweater.)
  - To make passive voice(Small fish *are* eaten by big fish.)
- *Have*
  - To make perfect tenses (I *have* finished my homework.)
- *Do*
  - To make negatives (I *do* not read novels.)
  - To ask questions *(Do* you read novels?)
  - To show emphasis (I *do* want you to read this novel.)
  - To stand for a main verb in some constructions (He reads faster than she *does*.)

Modal helping verbs

Modal helping verbs 'modify' the meaning of the main verb. A modal helping verb expresses necessity or possibility, and changes the main verb in that sense. The following are the modal verbs:

- can, could
- may, might
- will, would
- shall, should
- must
- ought to

Here are examples of using modal verbs:

- I *can't* speak French.
- The train *may* be late.
- *Would* you like to go for a picnic?
- You *should* see a doctor.
- I really *must* go now.

Main Verbs

Consider the below sentences:

- I *read*.
- People *read*.
- The sun *rises*.

From the above sentences, the meaning can be easily made out. That's because these verbs are *main verbs* and have a meaning on their own. They tell us something. There are thousands of main verbs.

In the following table, there are examples representing helping verbs and main verbs. Notice that all of these sentences have a main verb. Only some of them have a helping verb.

	Helping verb	Main verb	
Tanya		enjoys	music
You		enjoyed	music
They		are	Indians
The girls	are	watching	TV
We	must	go	now
I	do	read	poems

Linking Verbs

A linking verb is not quite meaningful in itself. It 'links' the subject to what is said about the subject. Usually, a linking verb shows equality (=) or a change to a different state or place (>). Linking verbs are always intransitive. However it should be kept in mind that all intransitive verbs are not linking verbs.

- Mahesh *is* a pilot. (Mahesh = pilot)
- The girl *is* beautiful. (The girl= beautiful)
- That *sounds* interesting. (That = interesting)
- The evening *became* pleasant. (The evening > pleasant)
- His throat *has gone* sour. (Throat > sour)

Dynamic and static verbs

Some verbs describe action and are called 'dynamic'. They can be used with continuous tenses. Other verbs describe state (non-action, a situation) and are called 'static', and cannot normally be used with continuous tenses (though some of them can be used with continuous tenses with a change in meaning).

Examples of Dynamic verbs:

- hit, explode, fight, run, go

Examples of Static verbs:

- be
- like, love, prefer, wish
- impress, please, surprise
- hear, see, sound
- belong to, consist of, contain, include, need
- appear, resemble, seem

Regular and irregular verbs

Regular and irregular verbs end differently from their past tense and past participle forms. For regular verbs, the past tense ending and past participle ending is always the same: -ed. For irregular verbs, the past tense ending and the past participle ending is variable.

Regular verbs:

base	*past tense*	*past participle*
• look	looked	looked
• work	worked	worked

Irregular verbs:

base	*past tense*	*past participle*
• buy	bought	bought
• cut	cut	cut
• do	did	done

Verb forms

English main verbs—except the verb 'to be'—have only 4, 5 or 6 forms. 'To be' has 9 forms.

All helping verbs are used with a main verb (either expressed or understood). There are 2 groups of helping verbs:

• *Tense helping verbs* are used to change the tense of the main verb.

• *Modal helping verbs* are used to change the 'mood' of the main verb.

Tense and Helping Verb		Modal Helping Verbs	
do	(to make simple tense)	can	could

Contd....

be	(to make continuous tense)	may	Might
have	(to make perfect tense)	will	Would
		shall	Should
		must	
		ought (to)	

Note: 'Do', 'be' and 'have' can also function as main verbs.

Modal helping verbs cannot function as main verbs.

Sometimes we make a sentence that has a helping verb and seems to have no main verb. In fact, the main verb is 'understood'. Consider the following examples:

- Question: *Can* you *play* piano? (The main verb *play* is 'expressed'.)
- Answer: Yes, I *can*. (The main verb *play* is not expressed. It is 'understood' from the context. We understand: Yes, I *can play* piano.

But, if somebody walks into the room and says, 'Hello. I can', nothing will be understood.

Tense

Tense is a method that we use to refer to time—past, present and future.

Tense and Time

It is important not to confuse the *name* of a verb tense with the way we use it to talk about *time*.

For example, a *present tense* does not always refer to *present time*:

- I hope it *rains* tomorrow. Here, 'rains' is present simple tense, but it refers here to a future time (tomorrow).

Or a *past tense* does not always refer to *past time*:

- If I *had* some time, I could have gone for the movie. Here, 'had' is past simple tense, but it refers here to a present time (now).

The following examples show how different tenses can be used to talk about different times.

Present Simple

Present - I *want* a candy.

Future - I will *leave* tomorrow.

He *likes* cakes.

Present Continuous

Present - I *am talking* on phone.

Future - I *am taking* my exam next month.

They *are studying* in America.

Present Perfect Simple

Past - I *have seen* him in the garden yesterday.

Present - I *have finished*.

Present Perfect Continuous

Past - I *have been reading* poetry.

Present - We *have been studying* for four hours.

Past Simple

Past - I *finished* one hour ago.

Present - If she *studied* now, she would clear the examination.

Future - If you *came* tomorrow, you would see her.

Past Continuous

Past - I *was working* till 2 am this morning.

Past Perfect Simple

Past - I *had* not *seen* him for quite a few days.

Past Perfect Continuous

Past - We *had been working* for 3 hours.

Present - If I *had been sleeping* now, I would have missed the opportunity.

Future - If I *had been working* tomorrow, I could not have agreed.

Future Simple

Present - Hold on. I'*ll do* it now.

Future - I'*ll see* you tomorrow.

Future Continuous

Future - I *will be going to the party* at 9 pm tonight.

Future Perfect Simple

Future - I *will have finished* by 9 pm tonight.

Future Perfect Continuous

Future - They may be tired when you arrive because they *will have been working*.

English tense system

For past and present, there are 2 simple tenses + 6 complex tenses (using auxiliary verbs). To these, we can add 4 'modal tenses' for the future (using modal auxiliary verbs will/shall). This makes a total of 12 tenses in the active voice. Another 12 tenses are available in the passive voice. So, we have 24 tenses.

The *use* of tenses in English may be quite complicated, but the *structure* of English tenses is actually very simple. The basic structure for a positive sentence is: Subject + auxiliary verb + main verb.

An auxiliary verb is used in all tenses. (In the simple present and simple past tenses, the auxiliary verb is usually suppressed for the affirmative, but it can and does exist for intensification.)

Technically, there are *no* future tenses in English. The word *will* is a modal auxiliary verb and future tenses are sometimes called 'modal tenses'.

Regular verbs

Following is the example of the *basic* English tense system with the regular verb *to play*. It includes the affirmative or positive form (+), the negative form (-) and the interrogative or question form (?).

The basic structure is:

+   Positive: Subject + auxiliary verb + main verb

            Negative: Subject + auxiliary verb + not + main verb

            Question: Auxiliary verb + subject + main verb

These are the various forms of the main verb that we use to construct the various tenses:

base verb	past	past participle	present participle -ing
play	played	played	playing

Tenses		Past	Present	Future
Simple do + base verb (except future: will + base verb)	+	I did play. I played.	I do play. I play.	I will play.
	-	I did not play.	I do not play.	I will not play.
	?	Did I play?	Do I play?	Will I play?

Contd....

Simple Perfect have + past participle	+	I had played.	I have played.	I will have played.
	-	I had not played.	I have not played.	I will not have played.
	?	Had I played?	Have I played?	Will I have played?
Continuous be + ing	+	I was playing.	I am playing.	I will be playing.
	-	I was not playing.	I am not playing?	I will not be playing.
	?	Was I playing?	Am I playing?	Will I be playing?
Continuous Perfect have been + ing	+	I had been playing.	I have been playing.	I will have been playing.
	-	I had not been playing.	I have not been playing.	I will not have been playing.
	?	Had I been playing?	Have I been playing?	Will I have been playing?

Irregular verbs

Following is the example of the *basic* English tense system with the irregular verb *to sing*. It includes the affirmative or positive form (+), the negative form (-) and the interrogative or question form (?).

The basic structure is:

+	Positive:	Subject + auxiliary verb + main verb
-	Negative:	Subject + auxiliary verb + not + main verb
?	Question:	Auxiliary verb + subject + main verb

These are the various forms of the main verb that we use to construct the various tenses:

Base verb	Past	Past participle	Present participle -ing
sing	sang	sung	singing

Tenses		Past	Present	Future
Simple do + base verb (except future: will + base verb)	+	I did sing. I sang.	I do sing. I sing.	I will sing.
	-	I did not sing.	I do not sing.	I will not sing.
	?	Did I sing?	Do I sing?	Will I sing?
Simple Perfect have + past participle	+	I had sung.	I have sung.	I will have sung.
	-	I had not sung.	I have not sung.	I will not have sung.
	?	Had I sung?	Have I sung?	Will I have sung?

Contd....

Continuous be + -ing	+	I was singing.	I am singing.	I will be singing.
	-	I was not singing.	I am not singing.	I will not be singing.
	?	Was I singing?	Am I singing?	Will I be singing?
Continuous Perfect have been + -ing	+	I had been singing.	I have been singing.	I will have been singing.
	-	I had not been singing.	I have not been singing.	I will not have been singing.
	?	Had I been singing?	Have I been singing?	Will I have been singing?

Irregular verb 'to be'

The tense system for the irregular verb *to be* includes the affirmative or positive form (+), the negative form (-) and the interrogative or question form (?). 'To be' is an exceptional verb. It is always different from other verbs, in various ways. The basic structure for *to be* is the same as for all verbs:

+   Positive: Subject + auxiliary verb + main verb

-     Negative: Subject + auxiliary verb + not + main verb

?   Question: Auxiliary verb + subject + main verb

Exception- For simple past and simple present tenses, the structure is not the same. In fact, it's even easier! There is *no* auxiliary verb. Here is the structure:

+   Positive: Subject + main verb

-     Negative: Subject + main verb + not

?   Question: Main verb + subject

These are the various forms of the main verb that we use to construct the various tenses:

Base	Past simple	Past participle	Present participle	Present simple
be	was, were	been	being	am, are, is

Tenses		Past	Present	Future
Simple *present simple* or *past simple* (except future: will + *base verb*)	+	I *was*.	I *am*.	I will *be*.
	-	I *was* not.	I *am* not.	I will not *be*.
	?	*Was* I?	*Am* I?	Will I *be*?
Simple Perfect have + *past participle*	+	I had *been*.	I have *been*.	I will have *been*.
	-	I had not *been*.	I have not *been*.	I will not have *been*.
	?	Had I *been*?	Have I *been*?	Will I have *been*?
Continuous be + *-ing*	+	I was *being*.	I am *being*.	I will be *being*.
	-	I was not *being*.	I am not *being*.	I will not be *being*.
	?	Was I *being*?	Am I *being*?	Will I be *being*?

Contd....

Continuous Perfect have been + -*ing*	+	I had been *being*.	I have been *being*.	I will have been *being*.
	-	I had not been *being*.	I have not been *being*.	I will not have been *being*.
	?	Had I been *being*?	Have I been *being*?	Will I have been *being*?

In the following table, *to be* is conjugated with all persons in the singular (I, you, he/she/it) and in the plural (we, you, they) for the 12 tenses.

Simple		Past	Present	Future
Singular	I	was	am	will be
	You	were	are	will be
	He/She/It	was	is	will be
Plural	We	were	are	will be
	You	were	are	will be
	They	were	are	will be
Singular	I	had been	have been	will have been
	You	had been	have been	will have been
	He/She/It	had been	has been	will have been
Plural	We	had been	have been	will have been

Contd....

	You	had been	have been	will have been
	They	had been	have been	will have been
Continuous		**Past**	**Present**	**Future**
Singular	I	was being	am being	will be being
	You	were being	are being	will be being
	He/She/It	was being	is being	will be being
Plural	We	were being	are being	will be being
	You	were being	are being	will be being
	They	were being	are being	will be being
Continuous Perfect		**Past**	**Present**	**Future**
Singular	I	had been being	have been being	will have been being
	You	had been being	have been being	will have been being
	He/She/It	had been being	has been being	will have been being
Plural	We	had been being	have been being	will have been being
	You	had been being	have been being	will have been being

Contd....

	They	had been being	have been being	will have been being

Simple Present Tense

I sing.

Rule:

Subject	+	Auxiliary verb	+	Main verb
		do		base

There are three important exceptions:

1. For positive sentences, *we do not normally use the auxiliary.*

2. For the 3rd person singular (he, she, it), we add *s* to the main verb or *es* to the auxiliary.

3. For the verb *to be*, we do not use an auxiliary, even for questions and negatives.

Look at these examples with the main verb *like*:

	Subject	Auxiliary verb		Main verb	
+	I, You, We, They			like	milkshake.
	He, She, It			likes	milkshake.
-	I, You, We, They	do	not	like	milkshake.
	He, She, It	does	not	like	milkshake.
?	Do	I, you, we, they		like	milkshake?
	Does	he, she, it		like	milkshake?

Look at these examples with the main verb *be*. Notice that there is no auxiliary:

	Subject	Main verb		
+	I	am		Indian.
	You, We, They	are		Indian.
	He, She, It	is		Indian.
-	I	am	not	tired.
	You, We, They	are	not	tired.
	He, She, It	is	not	tired.
?	Am	I		early?
	Are	you, we, they		early?
	Is	he, she, it		early?

Use of the Simple Present Tense

We use the simple present tense when:

- The action is general.
- The action happens all the time, or habitually, in the past, present and future.
- The action is not only happening now.
- The statement is always true.

For example:

- Neha *teaches* Geography.

- It *is* Neha's job to teach Geography.
- Neha does it every day.

Look at some more examples:

- I *live* in India.
- The Earth *goes around* the Sun.
- Joginder *drives* a taxi.
- He *does not drive* a scooter.
- We *go* to the church on every Sunday.
- Do you *enjoy* dancing?

Note that with the verb *to be*, we can also use the simple present tense for situations that are not general. We can use the simple present tense to talk about *now*. Look at these examples of the verb to be in the present simple tense—some of them are *general*, some of them are *now*:

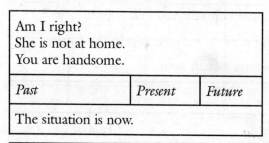

Am I right? She is not at home. You are handsome.		
Past	*Present*	*Future*
The situation is now.		

I am not angry. Why are you so sad? Ram is tall.		
Past	*Present*	*Future*
The situation is general. Past, present and future.		

Present Continuous Tense

I am working.

Rule:

The structure of the present continuous tense is:

Subject + Auxiliary verb + Main verb
　　　　　 Be　　　　　 base + ing

Look at these examples:

	Subject	Auxiliary verb		Main verb	
+	I	am		speaking	to you.
+	You	are		reading	this.
-	She	is	not	studying	in library.
-	We	are	not	playing	football.
?	Is	he		watching	movie?
?	Are	they		waiting	for John?

Use of the Present Continuous

We use the present continuous tense to talk about:

- Action happening now • Action in the future

a)　For action happening *exactly now*

I am eating my lunch.		
Past	*Present*	*Future*
	The action is happening now.	

b)　For action happening *around now*

The action may not be happening exactly now, but it is happening just before and just after now, and it is not permanent or habitual.

John is going out with Tanisha.		
Past	*Present*	*Future*
	The action is happening around now.	

Look at these examples:

- Neha *is learning* to swim.
- I *am living* with my sister until I find an apartment.

Present continuous tense for the future

Present continuous tense is employed only when we talk about the future when we have planned to do something before we speak. We must add (or understand from the context) a future word. 'Future words' include, for example, *tomorrow, next year, in June, at Christmas,* etc. It indicates that we have already *made a decision and a plan* before speaking.

I am visiting my aunt next month.		
Past	*Present*	*Future*
	A firm plan or programme exists now.	The action is in the future.

Look at these examples:

- We*'re eating* in a restaurant tonight. We've already booked the table.
- They can go to picnic with you tomorrow. They*'re* not *working*.
- When *are* you *starting* your new business?

In these examples, we have *a firm plan or programme before speaking*. The decision and plan were made *before* speaking.

We make the present continuous tense by adding -ing to the base verb. Normally it's simple—we just add -ing. However, at times, there is a little change in the words. Either we double the last letter, or we drop a letter. Here are the rules to help you know how to spell the present continuous tense.

Basic rule	Just add -ing to the base verb:		
	Work	>	Working
	Play	>	Playing
	Assist	>	Assisting
	See	>	Seeing
	Be	>	Being
Exception 1	If the base verb ends in consonant + stressed vowel + consonant, double the last letter:		
	s t o p vowel (vowels = a, e, i, o, u)		
	Stop	>	Stopping
	Run	>	Running
	Begin	>	Beginning
	Note that this exception does not apply when the last syllable of the base verb is not stressed		
	Open	>	Opening
Exception 2	If the base verb ends in *ie*, change the ie to y		
	Lie	>	Lying
	Die	>	Dying
Exception 3	If the base verb ends in vowel + consonant + *e*, omit the *e*:		
	Come	>	Coming
	Mistake	>	Mistaking

Present Perfect Tense

I have sung.

Rule:

The structure of the present perfect tense is:

Subject   +   Auxiliary verb   +   Main verb

                    Have   Past participle

Here are some examples of the present perfect tense:

	Subject	**Auxiliary verb**		**Main verb**	
+	I	have		seen	it.
+	You	have		eaten	pie.
-	She	has	not	been	to Rome.
-	We	have	not	played	football.
?	Have	you		finished?	
?	Have	they		done	it?

Use of the Present Perfect Tense

This tense is called the *present* perfect tense. There is always a connection with the past and with the *present*. There are basically three uses for the present perfect tense:

1.   Experience   2.   Change   3.   Continuing situation

Present perfect tense for experience

We often use the present perfect tense to talk *about experience* from the past.

I *have seen* it.
He *has studied* psychology in Japan.
Have you been there?
We *have never seen* him in the last few months.

Past	*Present*	*Future*
The action or state was in the past.	In my drawer, I *have a* copy of the novel now.	

Connection with past: the event was in the past.

Connection with present: in my head, *now*, I have a memory of the event; I *know* something about the event; I have *experience* of it.

Present perfect tense for change

Present perfect tense is also employed to talk about a *change* or *new* information:

I have bought a vase.		
Past	*Present*	*Future*
Last week I didn't have a vase.	Now I have a vase.	

Meena has broken her arm.		
Past	*Present*	*Future*
Yesterday Meena had a good arm.	Now she has a bad arm.	

Has the price gone up?		
Past	*Present*	*Future*
Was the price Rs. 280 yesterday?	Is the price Rs. 300 today?	

The police have arrested the killer.		
Past	*Present*	*Future*
Yesterday the killer was free.	Now the killer is in prison.	

Connection with past: the past is the opposite of the present.

Connection with present: the present is the opposite of the past.

Present perfect tense for continuing situation

We often use the present perfect tense to talk about a *continuing situation*. This is a state that started in the *past* and continues in the *present* (and will probably continue into the future). This is a *state* (not an action). We usually use *for* or *since* with this structure.

> I *have lived* here since June.
> He *has been ill* for 2 days.
> How long *have you known* him?

Past	Present	Future
The situation started in the past.	It continues up to now.	It will probably continue into the future.

Connection with past: the situation started in the past.

Connection with present: the situation continues in the present.

For and Since with Present Perfect

We often use *for* and *since* with the present perfect tense.

- We use *for* to talk about a *period* of time—15 minutes, 3 weeks, 6 years, etc.

- We use *since* to talk about *a point* in past time—9 o'clock, 1st January, Monday., etc.

For	Since
A period of time	*A point in past time*
24 minutes	5.00 pm
three days	Tuesday
6 months	January
4 years	1994
2 centuries	1800

| a long time | I left Delhi |
| ever | the beginning of time |

Here are some examples:

- I have been here *for* 20 minutes.
- I have been cooking *since* 10 in the morning.
- John hasn't called *for* 6 months.
- Viva hasn't written *since* December.
- He has worked in New York *for* a long time.
- He has lived in Delhi *since* childhood.

Present Perfect Continuous Tense
I have been swimming.

Rule:

The structure of the present perfect continuous tense is:

Subject +	Auxiliary verb +	Auxiliary verb +	Main verb
	have	been	base + ing
	has		

Contractions

When we use the present perfect continuous tense in speaking, we often contract the subject and the first auxiliary. At times, it is also done in the case of informal writing.

I have been	I've been
You have been	You've been
He has been	He's been
She has been	She's been
It has been	It's been
Neeta has been	Neeta's been
The bike has been	The bike's been

| We have been | We've been |
| They have been | They've been |

Here are some examples:

- I've been cooking.
- The car's been giving trouble.
- We've been watching the film for two and a half hours.

Use of the Present Perfect Continuous Tense

There is usually a connection with the *present* or now. There are basically two uses for the present perfect continuous tense:

1. An action that has just stopped or recently stopped

We use the present perfect continuous tense to talk about an *action* that started in the past and stopped recently. There is usually a result *now*.

I'm ill because I've been out in the cold.

| *Past* | *Present* | *Future* |
| Recent action. | Result now. | |

- I'm ill [now] because I've *been out in the cold*.
- Why is the grass wet [now]? *Has* it *been raining*?
- You don't score [now] because you *haven't been studying*.

2. An action continuing up to now

We use the present perfect continuous tense to talk about an *action* that started in the past and is continuing *now*. This is often used with *for* or *since*.

I have been enjoying music for 2 hours.

| *Past* | *Present* | *Future* |
| Action started in past. | Action is continuing now. | |

- I *have been enjoying music for* 2 hours. [I am still enjoying now.]

- We've *been studying since* 9 o'clock. [We're still studying now.]
- How long *have* you *been living in America*? [You are still living now.]
- We *have* not *been smoking*. [And we are not smoking now.]

Simple Past Tense

I swam.

Rule:

To make the simple past tense, we use:

- *Past form* only

  or

- Auxiliary *did* + *base form*

  Here you can see examples of the *past form* and *base form* for irregular verbs and regular verbs:

- He *drank* the milk.
- She *crossed* the road.
- The girl *kicked* the ball.
- The old man *did beat* the dog.
- *Did* they *see* the thief?

Past Continuous Tense

I was swimming.

Rule:

The structure of the past continuous tense is:

Subject	+	Auxiliary verb *be*	+	Main verb
		Conjugated in simple past tense		Present participle
		was		
		were		*base + ing*

For negative sentences in the past continuous tense, we insert *not* between the auxiliary verb and main verb. In the case of interrogative sentences, we exchange the *subject* and *auxiliary verb*. Look at these example sentences with the past continuous tense:

	Subject	Auxiliary verb		Main verb	
+	I	was		watching	TV.
+	You	were		studying	Geography.
-	He, She, It	was	not	helping	the police.
-	We	were	not	joking.	
?	Were	you		being	silly?
?	Were	they		attending	classes?

Use of the Past Continuous Tense

The past continuous tense expresses action at a *particular moment* in the past. The action started before that moment but has not finished at that moment. For example, Yesterday I watched a film on TV. The film started at 7pm and finished at 9 pm.

At 8 p.m. yesterday, I was watching TV.		
Past	*Present*	*Future*
At 8 pm, I was in the middle of watching TV.		

Look at these examples:

- I *was studying* at 10 pm last night.
- They *were* not *playing* football at 9 am this morning.
- What *were* you *doing* at 10 pm last night?
- What *were* you *doing* when the door bell rang?
- She *was knitting* when I telephoned her.

- We *were chatting* when it started to rain.
- All the roads from Shimla to Delhi were blocked because it *was snowing*.

Past Perfect Tense

I had sung.

Rule:

The structure of the past perfect tense is:

Subject	+	Auxiliary verb *have*	+	Main verb
		conjugated in simple past tense		past participle
		Had		base + *ed*

For negative sentences in the past perfect tense, we insert *not* between the auxiliary verb and main verb. For interrogative sentences, we exchange the *subject* and *auxiliary verb*. Look at these example sentences with the past perfect tense:

	Subject	Auxiliary verb		Main verb	
+	I	had		finished	my work.
+	You	had		arrived	earlier than me.
-	She	had	not	done	the job.
-	We	had	not	left.	
?	Had	you		written?	
?	Had	they		eaten	dinner?

Use of the Past Perfect Tense

The past perfect tense expresses action in the *past* before another action in the *past*. This is the *past in the past*. For example:

- The train left at 9 am. We arrived at 9.15 am. When we arrived, the train *had left*.

The train had left when we arrived.		
Past	*Present*	*Future*
Train leaves in past at 9 am.		
We arrive in past at 9.15 am.		

Look at some more examples:

- I wasn't hungry. I *had* just eaten bread.
- They were hungry. They *had* not *eaten* for five hours.
- I didn't know where he was. I *had* never *seen* him for five years.
- 'Mary wasn't at home when I arrived.'
  'Really? Where *had* she *gone*?'

Past Perfect Continuous Tense
I had been singing.

Rule:

The structure of the past perfect continuous tense is:

Subject	+	Auxiliary verb *have*	+	Auxiliary verb *be*	+	Main verb
		Conjugated in simple past tens		Past participle		Present participle
		Had		*been*		*base + ing*

For negative sentences in the past perfect continuous tense, we insert *not* after the first auxiliary verb. For question sentences, we exchange the *subject* and *first auxiliary verb*. Look at these example sentences with the past perfect continuous tense:

	Subject	Auxiliary verb		Auxiliary verb	Main verb	
+	I	had		been	working.	
+	You	had		been	knitting	a sweater.
-	It	had	not	been	working	well.
-	We	had	not	been	expecting	her.
?	Had	you		been	studying?	
?	Had	they		been	waiting	long?

Use of the Past Perfect Continuous Tense

The past perfect continuous tense is like the past perfect tense, but it expresses longer actions in the *past* before another action in the *past*. For example:

- Raman started studying at 9 am. His tutor arrived at 11am. When she arrived, Raman *had been studying* for two hours.

Raman had been studying for two hours when she arrived.		
Past	*Present*	*Future*
Raman started studying in past at 9 am.		
His tutor arrived in past at 11 am.		

- Neeta was very tired. She *had been jogging*.
- I could smell cigarettes. Somebody *had been smoking*.
- Suddenly, my car broke down. I was not surprised. It *had* not *been running* well for a long time.
- *Had* the driver *been drinking* before the accident?

Simple Future Tense
I will sing.

Rule:

The structure of the simple future tense is:

Subject + Auxiliary verb *will* + Main verb

Invariable   base

will   *base verb*

In case of negative sentences in the simple future tense, we insert *not* between the auxiliary verb and main verb. For interrogative sentences, we exchange the *subject* and *auxiliary verb*. Look at these example sentences with the simple future tense:

	Subject	Auxiliary verb		Main verb	
+	I	will		open	the door.
+	You	will		sing	before me.
-	She	will	not	be	at school tomorrow.
-	We	will	not	leave	yet.
?	Will	you		arrive	on time?
?	Will	they		want	tea?

Use of the Simple Future Tense

Simple future tense for No Plan

We use the simple future tense when there is no plan or decision to do something before we speak. Thus, the decision is made spontaneously at the time of speaking. Look at these examples:

- Hold on. I'*ll call* him.
- We *will see* what we can do to help you.
- Maybe we'*ll stay in* and *watch* snow fall on the hills from the window glass.

In all these examples, we had no firm plan before speaking. The decision is made *at the time of speaking*.

The use of the simple future tense with the verb *to think* before it is also very frequent:

- I *think* I'll go to the library.
- I *think* I will go on a holiday next year.
- I don't *think* I'll buy that car.

Simple future tense for Prediction

Simple future tense is also used to make a prediction about the future. Again, there is no firm plan. We are saying *what we think will happen*. Here are some examples:

- It *will rain* tomorrow.
- People *won't go* to Jupiter before the 22nd century.
- Who do you think they *will* vote for you?

Simple future tense with 'Be'

When the main verb is *be*, we can use the simple future tense even if we have a firm plan or decision before speaking. Examples:

- I'*ll be* in London tomorrow.
- I'm going to the market. I *won't be* very long.
- *Will* you *be* at work tomorrow?

Future Continuous Tense

I will be singing.

Rule:

The structure of the future continuous tense is:

Subject	+	Auxiliary verb *will*	+	Auxiliary verb *be*	+	Main verb
		Invariable		Invariable		Present participle
		will		*be*		base + *ing*

In case of negative sentences in the future continuous tense, we insert *not* between *will* and *be*. For interrogative sentences, we exchange the *subject* and *will*.

Use of the Future Continuous Tense

The future continuous tense expresses action at a *particular moment* in the future. The action will start before that moment but it will not have finished at that moment. For example, tomorrow I *will start* work at 2 pm and finish it by 6 pm.

At 4 pm tomorrow, she will be walking the ramp in Paris.		
Past	*Present*	*Future*
		At 4 pm, she will be in the middle of working.

Whenever the future continuous tense is employed, the listener usually knows or understands what time is being talked about. Look at these examples:

- I *will be playing* tennis at 11 am tomorrow.
- They *won't be reading newspaper* at 9 am in the morning.
- What *will* you *be doing* at 11 pm tonight?
- What *will* you *be doing* when I make a call?
- She *will* not *be sleeping* when you telephone her.
- We'll *be chatting on phone* when the film starts.
- Take your umbrella. It *will be raining* when you return.

Future Perfect Tense
I will have swum.

The *future perfect tense* is an easy tense to understand and use. The future perfect tense talks about the *past in the future*.

Rule:

The structure of the future perfect tense is:

Subject +	Auxiliary verb +	Auxiliary verb +	Main verb
	will	have	
	invariable	**invariable**	**past participle**
	will	*have*	*Third form*

Use of the Future Perfect Tense

The future perfect tense is used to represent an action in the future *before* another action in the future. This is the *past in the future*. For example:

The train reaches the platform at 9 am. You will arrive at the station at 9.15am. When you arrive, the train *will have left*.

The train will have left when you arrive		
Past	*Present*	*Future*
		Train leaves in future at 10 am.
		You arrive in future at 10.15 am.

Look at some more examples:

- You can call me at work at 8 am. I *will have arrived* at the office by 8.
- They will be tired when they arrive. They *will* not *have slept* for a long time.
- She won't be at home when her husband comes back. She *will have gone* to her aunt's.

Future Perfect Continuous Tense
I will have been painting.

Rule:

The structure of the future perfect continuous tense is:

Subject +	Auxiliary + verb *will*	Auxiliary + verb *have*	Auxiliary + verb *be*	Main verb
	invariable	invariable	past participle	present participle
	will	have	been	base + ing

As far as negative sentences in the future perfect continuous tense are concerned, we insert *not* between *will* and *have*. For interrogative sentences, we exchange the *subject* and *will*.

Use of the Future Perfect Continuous Tense

Future perfect continuous tense is used to talk about a long action before some point in the future. Look at these examples:

- I *will have been working* here for ten years next week.
- He will be quite happy when he arrives. He *will have been meeting* his parents after a very long span of time.

Nouns

A noun is defined as name of *a person, place or thing*. Here are some examples:

- *Person:* man, woman, teacher, Paras, Mala
- *Place:* home, office, town, countryside, Ambala
- *Thing:* table, car, banana, money, music, love, dog, monkey, apple

  A noun can be recognised in one of the following manner:

- Ending   •   Position
- Function

Noun Ending

There are certain word endings that show that a word is a noun, for example:

- -ity > *nationality*
- -ment > *appointment*
- -ness > *happiness*
- -ation > *relation*
- -hood > *childhood*

But this is not true for the word endings of all nouns. For example, the noun 'spoonful' ends in -ful, but the adjective 'careful' also ends in -ful.

Position in Sentence

A noun can often be recognised by its position in the sentence.

Nouns are often placed after a determiner. (A 'determiner' is a word like a, an, the, this, my, such.)

- a *rebuke*
- an *afternoon*
- the *architect*
- this *word*
- my *house*
- such *stupidity*

Nouns are often placed after one or more adjectives.

- a great *relief*
- a beautiful *afternoon*
- the tall, Indian *doctor*
- this difficult *essay*
- my brown and white *car*
- such crass *stupidity*

Function in a Sentence

Nouns have certain functions (jobs) in a sentence, for example:

- subject of verb > *Doctors* work hard.
- object of verb > He likes *coffee*.
- subject and object of verb > *Teachers* teach *students*.

But the subject or object of a sentence is not always a noun. It could be a pronoun or a phrase. In the sentence 'My teacher teaches well', the noun is 'teacher' but the subject is 'My teacher'.

Countable and Uncountable Nouns

Nouns are often described as 'countable' or 'uncountable'.

Countable Nouns

Countable nouns are easily recognised. They are things that we can count. For example: 'book'. We can count books. We can have one, two, three or more books. Here are some more countable nouns:

- dog, cat, animal, man, person
- bottle, box, litre
- coin, note, dollar
- cup, plate, fork
- table, chair, suitcase, bag

Countable nouns can be singular or plural:

- My *cat is* playing.
- My *cats are* playing.

We can use the indefinite article *a/an* with countable nouns:

- *A* peacock is *a* bird.

When a countable noun is singular, we must use a word like *a/the/my/this* with it:

- I need *an* umbrella. (*not* I need umbrella.)
- Where is *my* watch? (*not* Where is watch?)

When a countable noun is plural, we can use it alone:

- I read novels.
- Bottles can break.

Uncountable Nouns

Uncountable nouns are substances, concepts etc. that we cannot divide into separate elements. We cannot 'count' them. For example, we cannot count 'juice'. We can count 'bottles of juice' or 'litres of juice', but we cannot count 'juice' itself. Here are some more uncountable nouns:

- music, art, love, happiness
- advice, information, news
- furniture, luggage
- rice, sugar, butter, water
- electricity, gas, power
- money, currency

We usually treat uncountable nouns as singular. We use a singular verb. For example:

- *The information* received by us was crucial to the development of the strategy.
- Your luggage *looks* heavy.

We do not usually use the indefinite article *a/an* with uncountable nouns. We cannot say 'an information' or 'a music'. But we can say *a something of*:

- *a piece of* news
- *a bottle of* water
- *a grain of* rice

Nouns that can be Countable and Uncountable

Sometimes, the same noun can be countable *and* uncountable, often with a change of meaning.

Countable	Noun	Uncountable
There are two lights in our bedroom.	light	Draw the curtain. There's too much light!
Shhhhh! I thought I heard a noise.	noise	It's difficult to work when there is too much noise.
Have you got a paper to read?	paper	I want to draw a picture. Have you got some papers?
Our house has seven rooms.	room	Is there room for me to sit here?
We had a great time at the party.	time	Have you got time for a coffee?
Macbeth is one of Shakespeare's greatest works.	work	I have no money. I need work!

Adjectives

They add information to a sentence and tell us more about nouns and pronouns.

Determiners: A, An or The

The and *a/an* are called 'articles'. We divide them into 'definite' and 'indefinite' in the following manner:

Articles

Definite   Indefinite

The   A, An

We use 'definite' to mean sure, certain. 'Definite' is particular.

We use 'indefinite' to mean not sure, not certain. 'Indefinite' is general.

When we are talking about one thing in particular, we use *the*. When we are talking about one thing in general, we use *a* or *an*.

Think of the sky at night. In the sky there is one moon and millions of stars. So normally we could say:

- I saw *the* moon last night.
- I saw *a* star last night.

Now, think of a garden with a number of flowers and a gardener. You can say:

- I saw the gardener watering *the* plants.
- He won't let you pluck *a* single flower.

Look at these examples:

The

- *The* capital of France is Paris.
- I have found *the* book that I lost.
- Have you cleaned *the* car?
- There are six eggs in *the* fridge.
- Please switch off *the* TV when you finish.

A, An

- I was born in *a* town.
- John had *an* omelet for lunch.
- James Bond ordered *a* drink.
- We want to buy *an* umbrella.
- Have you got *a* pen?

We can use *The* or *A/An* for the same word. It depends on the situation.

Look at these examples:

- We want to buy *an* umbrella. (Any umbrella, not a particular umbrella.)
- Where is *the* umbrella? (We already have an umbrella. We are looking for our umbrella, a particular umbrella.)

Determiners: Each, Every

Each and *every* have similar but not always identical meanings. Verbs with *each* and *every* are always conjugated in the singular.

Each = every one separately.

Every = each, all.

Sometimes, *each* and *every* have the same meaning:

- Prices go up *each* year.
- Prices go up *every* year.

But often they are not exactly the same.

Each expresses the idea of 'one by one'. It emphasises individuality.

Every is half-way between each and all. It sees things or people as singular, but in a group or in general.

Consider the following examples:

- *Every* artist is imaginative.
- *Each* artist sees things differently.
- *Every* courtier bowed when the Sultan arrived.
- The principal gave *each* participant a certificate.
- *Each* participant received a souvenir.

Each can be used in front of the verb:

- The soldiers *each* received a certificate.

Each can be followed by 'of':

- The principal spoke to *each* of the students.
- He gave a certificate to *each* of them.

Every cannot be used for two things. For two things, *each* can be used:

- He was carrying a suitcase in *each* hand.

Every is used to say how often something happens:

- There is a plane to Mumbai *every* day.
- The bus leaves *every* hour.

Determiners: Some and Any

Some = a little, a few or a small number or amount

Any = one, some or all

Usually, we use *some* in **positive** (+) sentences and *any* in **negative** (-) and **question** (?) sentences.

	Some	Any	Example
+	I have some money.		I have Rs.30.
-		I don't have any money.	I don't have Rs. 30 and I don't have Rs.50 and I don't have Rs. 3,000,000. I have Rs.0.
?		Do you have any money?	Do you have Re. 1or Rs.10 or Rs. 1,000,000?

In general, we use *something/anything* and *somebody/anybody* in the same way as *some/any*.

Look at these examples:

- He needs *some* stamps.
- I must go. I have *some* homework to do.

- I'm thirsty. I want *something* to drink.
- I can see *somebody* coming.
- He doesn't need *any* stamps.
- I can stay. I don't have *any* homework to do.
- I'm not thirsty. I don't want *anything* to drink.
- I can't see *anybody* coming.
- Does he need *any* stamps?
- Do you have *any* homework to do?
- Do you want *anything* to drink?
- Can you see *anybody* coming?

We use *any* in a positive sentence when the <u>real sense is negative</u>.

- I refused to give them *any* money. (= I did <u>not</u> give them *any* money).
- She finished the test without *any* difficulty. (= she did <u>not</u> have *any* difficulty).

Sometimes we use *some* in a question, when we expect a <u>positive 'YES' answer</u>. (We could say that it is not a real question, because we think we know the answer already.)

- Would you like *some* more tea?
- Could I have *some* sugar, please?

Adjective Order

There are 2 basic positions for adjectives:

Before the *noun*

After certain *verbs* (be, become, get, seem, look, feel, sound, smell, taste)

	Adjective	Noun	Verb	Adjective
I like	spacious	cars.		
		My car	is	spacious.

Adjective before Nouns

We sometimes use more than one adjective before the noun:

- I like *big* black cars.
- She was wearing a *beautiful long red* dress.

What is the correct order for two or more adjectives?

1   The general order is: *opinion* => *fact*:

- A nice French car (not 'a French nice car')

('Opinion' is what you *think* about something. 'Fact' is what is definitely *true* about something.)

2.   The normal order for fact adjectives is replace, with =>

- a big, old, square, black, wooden Chinese table

3   Determiners usually come *first*, even though they are fact adjectives:

- Articles (a, the)
- Possessives (my, your...)
- Demonstratives (this, that...)
- Quantifiers (some, any, few, many...)
- Numbers (one, two, three)

When we want to use two *colour adjectives*, we join them with 'and':

- These days, newspapers are no more *black* and *white*.
- The dress was shaded *red*, *pink* and *yellow*.

These rules are not always rigid. Consider the following conversations:

Conversation 1

A   I want to buy a round table.

B   Do you want a new round table or an old round table?

Conversation 2

A   I want to buy an old table.

B   Do you want a round old table or a square old table?

Adjective after Verb

We can use an *adjective* after certain *verbs*. Even though the adjective is after the verb, it does not describe the verb. It describes the subject of the verb (usually a noun or pronoun).

For example:

Subject *verb adjective*

- Ram *is kind*.
- Because she had to wait, she *became impatient*.
- Is it *getting* gloomy?
- The examination did not *seem difficult*.
- Your friend *looks* happy.
- This towel *feels damp*.
- That new film doesn't *sound* very *interesting*.
- Dinner *smells good* tonight.
- This milk *tastes sour*.

Comparative Adjectives

When we talk about two things, we can 'compare' them. We can see if they are the same or different. Perhaps they are the same in some ways and different in other ways.

We can use comparative adjectives to describe the differences. For eg. Ratan is *taller* than Jatin.

Formation of Comparative Adjectives

There are two ways to form a comparative adjective:

- *Short* adjectives: add '*-er*' • *Long* adjectives: use '*more*'

Short adjective	
1-syllable adjectives	old, fast
2-syllable adjectives ending in -y	happy, easy
Normal rule: add '-er'	old > older
Variation: if the adjective ends in -e, just add -r	late > later
Variation: if the adjective ends in consonant, vowel, consonant, double the last consonant	big > bigger
Variation: if the adjective ends in -y, change the -y to -I	happy > happier
Long adjectives	
2-syllable adjectives not ending in -y	modern, pleasant
all adjectives of 3 or more syllables	expensive, intellectual
Normal rule: use 'more'	modern > more modern expensive >
	more expensive

Tip

With some 2-syllable adjectives, we can use '-er' *or* 'more':

- quiet > quieter/more quiet
- clever > cleverer/more clever
- narrow > narrower/more narrow
- simple > simpler/more simple

Exceptions

The following adjectives have irregular forms:

- good > better
- bad > worse
- far > farther/further

Use of Comparative Adjectives

Comparative adjectives are used when talking about two things. Often, the comparative adjective is followed by 'than'.

Look at these examples:

- Rekha is *prettier* than Neha.

    America is big. But Russia is *bigger*.

- I want to have a *more powerful* computer.
- Is French *more difficult* than English?

If we talk about the two planets Earth and Mars, we can compare them like this:

	Earth	Mars	
Diameter (km)	12,760	6,790	Mars is *smaller* than the Earth.
Distance from Sun (million km)	150	228	Mars is *more distant* from the Sun.
Length of day (hours)	24	25	A day on Mars is slightly *longer* than a day on the Earth.
Moons	1	2	Mars has *more* moons than the Earth.
Surface temperature (°C)	22	-23	Mars is *colder* than the Earth.

Superlative Adjectives

Superlative adjectives are used to compare more than two entities.

He is the *smartest* boy in the class.

Formation of Superlative Adjectives

As with comparative adjectives, there are two ways to form a *superlative adjective*:

- *short* adjectives: add '*-est*'
- *long* adjectives: use '*most*'

We also usually add 'the' at the beginning.

Short adjectives	
1-syllable adjectives	old, fast
2-syllable adjectives ending in -y	happy, easy
Normal rule: add '-est'	old > the oldest
Variation: if the adjective ends in -e, just add -st	late > the latest
Variation: if the adjective ends in consonant, vowel, consonant, double the last consonant	big > the biggest
Variation: if the adjective ends in -y, change the -y to -I	happy > the happiest

Contd....

Long adjectives	
2-syllable adjectives not ending in -y	modern, pleasant
all adjectives of 3 or more syllables	expensive, intellectual
Normal rule: use 'most'	modern > the most modern expensive > the most expensive

Tip

With some 2-syllable adjectives, we can use '-est' *or* 'most':

* quiet > the quietest/most quiet
* clever > the cleverest/most clever
* narrow > the narrowest/most narrow
* simple > the simplest/most simple

Exceptions

The following adjectives have irregular forms:

* good > the best
* bad > the worst
* far > the furthest

Use of Superlative Adjectives

We use a superlative adjective to describe one thing in a group of three or more things.

Look at these examples:

* Megha is *pretty*. Radhika is *prettier*. Sheena is *prettiest*.
* Amit, Sachin and Rahul are *rich* businessmen. But, Sachin is the *richest*.
* Mount Everest is *the highest* mountain in the world.

If we talk about the three planets Earth, Mars and Jupiter, we can
use superlatives like this:

	Earth	Mars	Jupiter	
Diameter (km)	12,760	6,790	142,800	Jupiter is *the biggest.*
Distance from Sun (million km)	150	228	778	Jupiter is *the most distant* from the Sun.
Length of day (hours)	24	25	10	Jupiter has *the shortest* day.
Moons	1	2	16	Jupiter has *the most* moons.
Surface temperature (°C)	22	-23	-150	Jupiter is *the coldest.*

Adverbs

An *adverb* is a word that reveals more about a verb. An adverb
'qualifies' or 'modifies' a *verb* (The man *worked faster*). But adverbs
can also modify *adjectives* (She is *really efficient*), or even other
adverbs (It works *very well*).

Different kinds of word are called adverbs. We can usually
recognise an adverb by its:

1. Function (Job)
2. Form
3. Position

Function

The principal job of an adverb is to modify (give more
information about) verbs, adjectives and other adverbs. In the

following examples, the adverb is *italicised* and the word that it modifies is <u>underlined</u>.

- Modify a verb:
  - She <u>speaks</u> *fluently*. (How does she speak?)
  - Megha <u>lives</u> *nearby*. (Where does Megha live?)
  - She *never* <u>drinks</u>. (Does she drink?)
- Modify an adjective:
  - He is *really* <u>intelligent</u>.
- Modify another adverb:
  - She drives *incredibly* <u>slowly</u>.

But, adverbs have other functions, too. They can:

- Modify a whole sentence:
  - *Obviously*, <u>I</u> <u>can't</u> <u>do</u> <u>everything</u>.
- Modify a prepositional phrase:
  - He went *immediately* <u>inside</u> <u>the</u> <u>room</u>.

Form

Many adverbs end in -ly. We form such adverbs by adding -ly to the adjective. Here are some examples:

- quickly, softly, strongly, honestly, interestingly

However, it should be noted that all the words that end in – ly are not adverbs. 'Friendly', for example, is an adjective.

Some adverbs have no particular form, for example:

- well, fast, very, never, always, often, still

Position

Adverbs have three main positions in a sentence:

- Front (before the subject):
  - *Now* we will study adverbs.

- Middle (between the subject and the main verb):
    - We *often* study adverbs.
- End (after the verb or object):
    - We study adverbs *carefully*.

Pronouns

Pronouns are often used to replace a noun. We can use a pronoun instead of a noun. Pronouns are words like: *he, you, ours, themselves, some, each*... If we didn't have pronouns, we would have to repeat a lot of nouns. We would have to say things like:

- Do you like the President? I don't like the President. The President is too pompous.

    With pronouns, we can say:

- Do you like the President? I don't like *her*. *She* is too pompous.

Prepositions

A *preposition* is a word governing, and usually coming in front of, a noun or pronoun and expressing a relation to another word or element, as in:

- She left *before* breakfast
- What did you come *for*?
- The cow is grazing in the field.

Here is a short list of some common one-word prepositions. But, it should be kept in mind that many of these prepositions have more than one meaning.

- aboard
- above
- after
- along

- about
- across
- against
- amid

- among
- around
- at
- behind
- beneath
- besides
- beyond
- by
- considering
- down
- except
- excluding
- for
- in
- into
- minus
- of
- on
- opposite
- over
- per
- regarding
- save
- than
- to
- towards
- underneath
- until
- upon
- anti
- as
- before
- below
- beside
- between
- but
- concerning
- despite
- during
- excepting
- following
- from
- inside
- like
- near
- off
- onto
- outside
- past
- plus
- round
- since
- through
- toward
- under
- unlike
- up
- versus

- via
- within
- with
- without

Preposition Rule

There is one very simple rule for using prepositions.

Rule

A preposition is followed by a 'noun'. It is never followed by a verb.

By 'noun' we include:

- *Noun* (dog, money, love)
- *Proper noun (name)* (Bangkok, Mary)
- *Pronoun* (you, him, us)
- *Noun group* (my first job)
- *Gerund* (swimming)

A preposition cannot be followed by a verb. If we want to follow a preposition by a verb, we must use the '-ing' form which is really a gerund or verb in noun form.

Here are some examples:

Subject + verb	Preposition	'Noun'
The food is	on	the table.
She lives	in	Japan.
Tara is looking	for	you.
The letter is	under	your blue book.
Stick is used	to	beat someone.
She isn't used	to	working.
I ate	before	coming.

Example:

In the following sentences, why is 'to' followed by a verb? That should be impossible, according to the rule:

• I would like to go now.
• She used to smoke.

Answer:

In these sentences, 'to' is *not* a preposition. It is part of the *infinitive* ('to go', 'to smoke').

Prepositions of Place: at, in, on

In general, we use:

• *at* for a Point
• *in* for an Enclosed space
• *on* for a Surface

At	In	On
Point	*Enclosed space*	*Surface*
at the corner	in the garden	on the wall
at the bus stop	in London	on the ceiling
at the door	in France	on the door
at the top of the page	in a box	on the cover
at the end of the road	in my pocket	on the floor
at the entrance	in my wallet	on the carpet
at the crossroads	in a building	on the menu
at the entrance	in a car	on a page

Look at these examples:

- Kanika is waiting for you *at* the bus stop.
- Their residence is *at* the end of the street.
- My plane stopped *at* Dubai and Hanoi and arrived *in* Bangkok two hours late.
- When is the chief guest going to arrive *at* the function?
- Do you work *in* an office?
- The conference is going to be held *in* New York.
- Do you live *in* Japan?
- Neptune is *in* the Solar System.
- You may find the name of the company *on* the label of the product.
- There are no prices *on* this menu.
- Don't cut the branch that you are sitting *on*.
- There was a 'no smoking' sign *on* the wall.

Notice the use of the prepositions of place *at*, *in* and *on* in these standard expressions:

At	In	On
at home	in a car	on a bus
at work	in a taxi	on a train
at school	in a helicopter	on a plane
at university	in a boat	on a ship
at college	in a lift (elevator)	on a bicycle, on a motorbike
at the top	in the newspaper	on a horse, on an elephant
at the bottom	in the sky	on the radio, on television
at the side	in a row	on the left, on the right
at reception	in Oxford Street	on the way

Prepositions of Time: at, in, on

We use:

- *at* for a precise time
- *in* for months, years, centuries and long periods
- *on* for days and dates

At	In	On
Precise time	*Months, years, centuries and long periods*	*Days and dates*
at 3 o'clock	in May	on Sunday
at 10.30 am	in summer	on Tuesdays
at noon	in the summer	on 6 March
at dinnertime	in 1990	on 25 Dec. 1964
at bedtime	in the 1990s	on Christmas Day
at sunrise	in the next century	on Independence Day
at sunset	in the Ice Age	on my birthday
at the moment	in the past/future	on New Year's Eve

Look at these examples:

- The examination begins *at* 9 am.
- The shop closes *at* midnight.
- She came back home *at* lunchtime.
- In England, it often snows *in* December.
- Do you think we will go to Jupiter *in* the future?
- You should have found a copy of the book *in* the library.

- Do you work *on* Mondays?
- Her birthday is *on* 20 November.
- Where will you be *at* 10 am tomorrow morning?

Conjunctions

Conjunctions are words that *join*. A conjunction joins two parts of a sentence.

Form

Conjunctions have three basic forms:

- *Single Word*

  For example: and, but, because, although

- *Compound* (often ending with *as* or *that)*

  For example: provided that, as long as, in order that

- *Correlative* (which surround an adverb or adjective)

  For example: so...that

Function (Job)

Conjunctions are divided into two basic types.

- *Coordinating Conjunctions* are used to join two parts of a sentence that are grammatically equal. The two parts may be single words or clauses, for example:

  - <u>Jack</u> *and* <u>Jill</u> went up the hill.

  - <u>The weather was pleasant</u> *but* <u>I didn't go for the picnic</u>.

- *Subordinating Conjunctions* are used to join a subordinate dependent clause to a main clause, for example:

  - <u>I went swimming</u>, *although* <u>it was cold</u>.

Coordinating conjunctions always come *between* the words or clauses that they join.

When a coordinating conjunction joins independent clauses, it is always correct to place a comma before the conjunction:

- I want to work as a lecturer in the future, *so* I have opted for an M.Phil programme.

However, if the independent clauses are short and well-balanced, a comma is not really essential:

- She is generous *so* she donates for charity.

When 'and' is used with the last word of a list, a comma is optional:

- He drinks beer, whisky, wine, *and* rum.
- He drinks beer, whisky, wine *and* rum.

Subordinating Conjunctions

The majority of conjunctions are 'subordinating conjunctions'. Common subordinating conjunctions are:

- after, although, as, because, before, how, if, once, since, than, that, though, till, until, when, where, whether, while

A subordinating conjunction joins a subordinate (dependent) clause to a main (independent) clause.

Look at this example:

Main or independent clause	Subordinate or dependent clause	
Ram went swimming	*although*	it was raining.
	Subordinating conjunction	

Interjections

Interjection is a big name for a little word. Interjections are short exclamations like *Oh!* *Um* or *Ah!* They have no real grammatical value but we use them quite often, usually more in speaking than in writing.

It should be kept in mind that when interjections are inserted into a sentence, they have no grammatical connection to the sentence. An interjection is sometimes followed by an exclamation mark (!).

Here are some interjections with examples:

Interjection	Meaning	Example
Ah	Expressing pleasure	'Ah, that feels good.'
	Expressing realisation	'Ah, now I understand.'
	Expressing resignation	'Ah well, it can't be hoped.'
	Expressing surprise	'Ah! I've won!'
Alas	Expressing grief or pity	'Alas, she's dead now.'
Dear	Expressing pity	'Oh dear! Does it hurt?'
	Expressing surprise	'Dear me! That's a surprise!'
Eh	Asking for repetition	'It's hot today.' 'Eh?' 'I said it's hot today.'
	Expressing enquiry	'What do you think of that, eh?'
	Expressing surprise	'Eh! Really?'
	Inviting agreement	'Let's go, eh?'
Er	Expressing hesitation	'Lima is the capital of...er...Peru.'

Contd....

Hello, hullo	Expressing greeting	'Hello John. How are you today?'
	Expressing surprise	'Hello! My car's gone!'
Hey	Calling attention	'Hey! Look at that!'
	Expressing surprise, joy etc	'Hey! What a good idea!'
Hi	Expressing greeting	'Hi! What's new?'
Hmm	Expressing hesitation, doubt or disagreement	'Hmm. I'm not so sure.'
Oh, o	Expressing surprise	'Oh! You're here!'
	Expressing pain	'Oh! I've got a toothache.'
	Expressing pleading	'Oh, please say 'yes'!'
Ouch	Expressing pain	'Ouch! That hurts!'
Uh	Expressing hesitation	'Uh...I don't know the answer to that.'
Uh-huh	Expressing agreement	'Shall we go?' 'Uh-huh.'
Um, umm	Expressing hesitation	'85 divided by 5 is...um...17.'
Well	Expressing surprise	'Well I never!'
	Introducing a remark	'Well, what did he say?'

CHAPTER 4

Improving Pronunciation

Pronouncing **every** word correctly leads to poor pronunciation! Good pronunciation comes from stressing the right words. This is because English is a **time-stressed** language. Here is how to do it:

1. Learn the rules concerning pronunciation thoroughly.

2. English is considered a stressed language while many other languages are considered syllabic.

3. In other languages, such as French or Italian, each syllable receives equal importance (there is stress, but each syllable has its own length).

4. English pronunciation focuses on specific stressed words while quickly gliding over the other, non-stressed, words.

5. Stressed words are considered **content words**: Nouns e.g. kitchen, Peter – (most) principle verbs e.g. visit, construct – Adjectives e.g. beautiful, interesting – Adverbs e.g. often, carefully

6. Non-stressed words are considered **function words**: Determiners e.g. the, a – Auxiliary verbs e.g. am, were – Prepositions e.g. before, of – Conjunctions e.g. but, and – Pronouns e.g. they, she

Read the following sentence aloud:

The beautiful mountain appeared transfixed in the distance.

Now, read the following sentence aloud:

He can come on Sundays as long as he doesn't have to do any homework in the evening.

Notice that the first sentence actually takes about the same time to speak well! Even though the second sentence is approximately 30% longer than the first, the sentences take the same time to speak. This is because there are 5 stressed words in each sentence.

Write down a few sentences, or take a few example sentences from a book or exercise. First underline the stressed words, then read aloud focusing on stressing the underlined words and gliding over the non-stressed words. When listening to native speakers, focus on how those speakers stress certain words and begin to copy this.

Tips on improving pronunciation

1. Remember that non-stressed words and syllables are often 'swallowed' in English.

2. Always focus on pronouncing stressed words well, non-stressed words can be glided over.

3. Do not focus on pronouncing each word. Focus on the stressed words in each sentence.

About word stress

Word stress is your magic key to understanding spoken English. Native speakers of English use word stress naturally. Word stress is so natural for them that they do not even know they use it. Non-native speakers who speak English to native speakers without using word stress, encounter two problems:

1. They find it difficult to understand native speakers, especially those speaking fast.

2. The native speakers find it difficult to understand them.

Understanding syllables

Understanding syllables helps to understand word stress. Every word is made from syllables. Each word has one, two, three or more syllables.

Word		Number of syllables
Dog	Dog	1
Green	Green	1
Quite	Quite	1
Quiet	Qui-et	2
Orange	O-range	2
Table	Ta-ble	2
Expensive	Ex-pen-sive	3
Interesting	In-ter-est-ing	4
Realistic	Re-a-lis-tic	4
Unexceptional	Un-ex-cep-tio-nal	5

Notice that (with a few rare exceptions) every syllable contains at least one vowel (a, e, i, o or u) or vowel sound.

Understanding word stress

In English, we do not say each syllable with the same force or strength. In one word, we accentuate one syllable. We say one syllable very loudly (big, strong, important) and all the other syllables very quietly.

Let us take three words: **photograph, photographer** and **photographic.** Do they sound the same when spoken? No. This is because one syllable in each word is accentuated (stressed), and it is not always the same syllable. So, the sound of each word is different:

Words	Total syllables	Stressed syllable
PHO TO GRAPH	3	#1
PHO **TO** GRAPH ER	4	#2
PHO TO **GRAPH** IC	4	#3

This happens in all words with two or more syllables: TEACHer, JaPAN, CHINa, aBOVE, converSAtion, INteresting, imPORtant, deMAND, etCETera, etCETera.

The syllables that are not stressed are 'weak' or 'small' or 'quiet'. Native speakers of English listen for the stressed syllables, not the weak syllables. If you use word stress in your speech, you will instantly and automatically improve your pronunciation and your comprehension.

Try to hear the stress in individual words each time you listen to English – on the radio, or in films for example. Your first step is to hear and recognise it. After that, you can use it!

There are two very important rules about word stress:

1. **One word, one stress.** One word cannot have two stresses. So if you hear two stresses, you have heard two words, not one word.

2. **The stress is always on a vowel.**

Importance of word stress

Word stress is not used in all languages. Some languages, Japanese or French for example, pronounce each syllable with eq-ual em-pha-sis.

Other languages, English for example, use word stress. Word stress is not an optional extra that you can add to the English language if you want. It is part of the language! English speakers use word stress to communicate rapidly and accurately, even in difficult conditions. If, for example, you do not hear a word clearly, you can still understand the word because of the position of the stress.

Think again about the two words **photograph** and **photographer**. Now imagine that you are speaking to somebody by telephone over a very bad line. You cannot hear clearly. In fact, you hear only the first two syllables of one of these words, **photo...** Which word is it, photograph or photographer? Of course, with word stress you will know immediately which word it is because in reality you will hear either **PHOto...** or **phoTO...** So, without hearing the whole word, you probably know what the word is (**PHOto...graph** or **phoTO...grapher**).

This is a simple example of how word stress helps us understand English. There are many, many other examples, because we use word stress all the time, without thinking about it.

Where to put word stress?

There are some rules about which syllable to stress. Though the rules are rather complicated, the best way to learn is from experience. Listen carefully to spoken English and try to develop a feeling for the 'music' of the language.

When you learn a new word, you should also learn its stress pattern. If you keep a vocabulary book, make a note to show which syllable is stressed. If you do not know, you can look in a dictionary. All dictionaries give the phonetic spelling of a word. This is where they show which syllable is stressed, usually with an apostrophe (') just **before** or just **after** the stressed syllable. (The notes at the front of the dictionary will explain the system used.) Look at this example for the word **plastic**. There are 2 syllables. Syllable #1 is stressed:

Example	Phonetic spelling: dictionary A	Phonetic spelling: dictionary B
PLAS TIC	/plæs'tIk/	/'plæs tIk/

Rules of word stress

There are few very simple rules about word stress:

1. **One word has only one stress.** (One word cannot have two stresses. If you hear two stresses, you hear two words. Two stresses cannot be one word. It is true that there can be a 'secondary' stress in some words. But a secondary stress is much smaller than the main [primary] stress, and is only used in long words.)

Examples

Rule	Example
Most **2-syllable nouns**	CHIna, TAble, EXport
Most **2-syllable adjectives**	SLENder, CLEVer, HAPpy

Stress on last syllable

Rule	Example
Most **2-syllableverbs**	to exPORT, to deCIDE, to beGIN

2. **Only vowels are stressed, not consonants.** Here are some more, rather complicated, rules that can help you understand where to put the stress. But do not rely on them too much, because there are many exceptions. It is better to try to 'feel' the music of the language and to add the stress naturally.

3.   Stress on penultimate syllable. Here, second last syllables are stressed.

Example

Rule	Example
Words ending in -ic	GRAPHic, geoGRAPHic, geoLOGic
Words ending in -sion and -tion	teleVIsion, reveLAtion

4.   Stress on ante-penultimate syllable. Here third last syllables are stressed.

Rule	Example
Words ending in -cy, -ty, -phy and -gy	deMOcracy, dependaBIlity, phoTOgraphy, geology
Words ending in -al	CRItical, geological

5.   Compound words. These are words with two parts.

Rule	Example
For compound **nouns,** the stress is on the **first** part	BLACKbird, GREENhouse
For compound **adjectives,** the stress is on the **second** part	bad-TEMpered, old-FASHioned
For compound **verbs,** the stress is on the **second** part	to underSTAND, to overflow

Sentence stress in English

Sentence stress is the music of spoken English. Like word stress, sentence stress can help you to understand spoken English, especially when spoken fast.

Sentence stress is what gives English its **rhythm** or 'beat'. You remember that word stress is accent on **one syllable** within a **word**. Sentence stress is accent on **certain words** within a **sentence**.

Most sentences have two types of words:

- Content words
- Structure words

Content words are the key words of a sentence. They are the important words that carry the meaning or sense.

Structure words are not very important words. They are small, simple words that make the sentence correct grammatically. They give the sentence its correct form or 'structure'.

If you remove the structure words from a sentence, you will probably still understand the sentence. If you remove the content words from a sentence, you will **not** understand the sentence. The sentence has no sense or meaning.

Imagine that you receive this telegram message:

Will you **SELL** me **CAR** because I'm **GONE** to **FRANCE**.

This sentence is not complete. It is not a 'grammatically correct' sentence. But you probably understand it. These four words communicate very well. Somebody wants you to **sell** their **car** for them because they have **gone** to **France**. We can add a few words:

Will you **SELL** my **CAR** because I've **GONE** to **FRANCE**.

The new words do not really add any more information. But they make the message more correct grammatically. We can add even more words to make one complete, grammatically correct sentence. But the information is basically the same. In the sentence, the four **key words** (sell, car, gone, France) are accentuated or stressed.

Sentence stress is important because it adds 'music' to the language. It is the **rhythm** of the English language. It changes the speed at which we speak (and listen to) the language. The time between each stressed word is the same.

In the example sentence, there is **one syllable** between **SELL** and **CAR** and **three syllables** between **CAR** and **GONE**. But the **time** (*t*) between **SELL** and **CAR** and between **CAR** and **GONE** is the same. A constant beat on the stressed words is maintained. To do this, we say 'my' more **slowly**, and 'because I've' more **quickly**. The speed of the small structure words is changed so that the rhythm of the key content words stays the same.

Syllables

2   1   3   1

Will you **SELL** my **CAR** because I've **GONE** to **FRANCE**.

Rules for sentence stress

The basic rules of sentence stress are:

1.   Content words are stressed

2.   Structure words are unstressed

3.   The time between stressed words is always the same

The following tables can help you decide which words are **content words** and which words are **structure words**:

Content words - stressed

Words carrying meaning	Example
Main verbs	sell, give, employ
Nouns	car, music, Mary
Adjectives	red, big, interesting
Adverbs	quickly, loudly, never
Negative auxiliaries	don't, aren't, can't

Structure words - unstressed

Words for correct grammar	Example
Pronouns	he, we, they
Prepositions	on, at, into
Articles	a, an, the
Conjunctions	and, but, because
Auxiliary verbs	do, be, have, can, must

Exceptions

The above rules are for what is called 'neutral' or normal stress. But sometimes we can stress a word that would normally be only a structure word, for example to correct the information. Look at the following dialogues:

- They've been to Mongolia, haven't they?
- No, **they** haven't, but **we** have.

Note also that when 'be' is used as a main verb, it is usually unstressed (even though in this case it is a content word).

Phonetic symbols

Phonetic symbols are a great help when it comes to learning to pronounce English words correctly. Any time you open a dictionary, you can find the correct pronunciation of words you do not know by looking at the phonetic pronunciation that follows the word. Unfortunately, learning the phonetic alphabet is not always the easiest thing to do.

In English, as you certainly know, many words can have the same pronunciation but are written differently and have different meanings. For example, 'to', 'two', and 'too', all have the phonetic transcription /tu/. Sometimes, words can be written similarly but have different pronunciations as in the 'ough' combinations thought, though, bough, and through. Another factor in pronunciation is the how the word is stressed. Understanding the phonetic alphabet can greatly simplify the learning process, especially for students who do not have the opportunity to work with a teacher.

The following table is an example of a text that has been transcribed in to phonetics. Notice how the text, as it would be spoken, differs from how each word might be transcribed individually. This is principally due to two factors: elision and unstressed syllables.

Consonants

Sound	Examples
p	pen, copy, happen
b	back, baby, job
t	tea, tight, button
d	day, ladder, odd
k	key, clock, school
g	get, giggle, ghost
tʃ	church, match, nature
dʒ	judge, age, soldier
f	fat, coffee, rough, photo
v	view, heavy, move
θ	thing, author, path
ð	this, other, smooth
s	soon, cease, sister
z	zero, music, roses, buzz
ʃ	ship, sure, national
ʒ	pleasure, vision
h	hot, whole, ahead
m	more, hammer, sum

n	nice, know, funny, sun
ŋ	ring, anger, thanks, sung
l	light, valley, feel
r	right, wrong, sorry, arrange
j	yet, use, beauty, few
w	wet, one, when, queen

Vowels

Sound	Examples
ɪ	kit, bid, hymn, minute
e	dress, bed, head, many
æ	trap, bad
ɒ	lot, odd, wash
ʌ	strut, mud, love, blood
ʊ	foot, good, put
iː	fleece, sea, machine
eɪ	face, day, break
aɪ	price, high, try
ɔɪ	choice, boy
uː	goose, two, blue, group
əʊ	goat, show, no
aʊ	mouth, now
ɪə	near, here, weary
eə	square, fair, various
ɑː	start, father
ɔː	thought, law, north, war
ʊə	poor, jury, cure
ɜː	nurse, stir, learn, refer
ə	about, common, standard
i	happy, radiate, glorious
u	thank you, influence, situation
n̩	suddenly, cotton
l̩	middle, metal
ˈ	(stress mark)

Note how the following text is pronounced using phonetic symbols:

Use phonetic symbols and transcribed the text given below. Note how the pronunciation comes out when you use the phonetic symbol.

There is a police message for motorists in the Barnet area of London. A lorry has shed its load at the Apex Corner roundabout on the A1. You are asked to avoid the area as much as possible. South-bound traffic will be diverted for the next two hours. That is the end of the message.

As you can see, the phonetic alphabet seems like another language entirely, however, with patience, it can serve you well in improving your pronunciation.

Chapter 5

Idioms for Better English Speaking

An idiom is a phrase, construction, or expression that is recognised as a unit in the usage of a given language and either differs from the usual syntactic patterns or has a meaning that differs from the literal meaning of its parts taken together.

From the definition it is quite evident that idioms are an integral part of English language speaking. Below are given a list of idioms along with their meanings and suitable illustrations.

Follow in someone's footsteps
(To follow someone's example; to do what another person has done.)

Example: Mike decided to follow in his father's footsteps and join the army.

A similar expression is *follow in someone's track.*

Bark is worse than one's bite
(Sound or speech is worse than actions.)

Example: Our history teacher is always yelling about people being late, but his bark is worse than his bite. He won't fail anyone just for being late a few times.

Bark up the wrong tree
(To choose the wrong person or course of action.)

Example: If you think I'm going to give you any money, you are barking up the wrong tree.

Bargain for

(To be ready for or to expect something.)

Example: The final cost for his children's college tuition was more than Bill bargained for.

Baloney

(Something that is nonsense, untrue or unbelievable.)

Example: John says he makes a lot of money at his new job, but I think it's a bunch of baloney.

Bad mouth someone

(To say something untrue or uncomplimentary about someone in order to damage their reputation.)

Example: It was very unprofessional for Jack to bad mouth his boss.

Back-to-back

(Immediately following.)

Example: One after another. I have five classes back-to-back on Thursdays.

Back talk

(A sassy or impudent reply.)

Example: Back talk like that will only get you into more trouble.

In demand

(Needed; wanted.)

Example: Bill's talent was so great that his services were soon in demand throughout the country

Jump the gun

(To start before you should)

Example: He jumped the gun and started selling the tickets before he should.

If you can't lick them, join them

(If you cannot defeat an opponent or get him to change his attitude, plans, or ways of doing things, the best thing to do is to change your ideas, plans, etc.)

Example: "The small car manufacturers are winning over the big car makers," the CEO of an American car factory said. "If we want to stay in business, we must do as they do. In other words, if you can't lick them, join them."

Jump through hoops

(To do whatever you are told to do; to obey an order)

Example: I had to jump through several hoops before I could get a visa to work overseas.

A similar expression is *play (someone's) game*.

Example: The immigration office likes to make people play their silly little games before giving out a visa to work abroad.

Jump on the bandwagon

(To join a popular cause or movement.)

Example: The Helpage India Foundation is a good cause. We want you to jump on the bandwagon with us by making a donation to the foundation.

Jump on

(To scold; to yell at)

Example: Sam jumped on Bill for being late for work.

Example: Susie jumped all over Micheal for coming home drunk.

Jump down one's throat

(To suddenly become very angry at someone; to scold severely or angrily.)

Example: The teacher jumped down Billy's throat when he said he didn't do his homework.

John Q. Public

(A name used informally for the average citizen.)

Example: It is John Q. Public's duty to vote in every election.

John Hancock

(Your signature; your name in writing.)

Example: The man said, "Just sign your John Hancock on this paper and the car will be all yours."

John Doe

(A name used for an unknown person, especially in police and law enforcement.)

Example: The detective stood quietly looking at the dead man lying on the ground. He was the second John Doe murdered that week.

Jack of all trades

[(often followed by the words 'master of none.') A person who is knowledgeable in many areas. Can be used as praise, or as a derogatory remark depending on the context and the intonation.]

Example: Peter is a jack of all trades; he can survive anywhere!

Example: "How come Bill did such a sloppy job?" Mary asked.

"You know Bill," Sally answered. "He's a jack of all trades, but a master of none. Next time you should hire a professional."

In spite of

(Against the influence or effect of; in opposition to; defying the effect of; despite.)

Example: In spite of the bad storm, John delivered his papers on time.

Example: In spite of all their differences, Joan and Ann remain friends.

In stitches

(Laughing so hard that the sides ache; in a fit of laughing hard.)

Example: The comedian was so funny that he had everyone in stitches.

Backseat driver

(A bossy person in a car who always tells the driver what to do.)

Example: I hate being in the car with my mother. She is such a backseat driver.

In one's shoes

(In or into one's place or position.)

Example: I was taught to never criticise a man until I'd been in his shoes.

In one's hair

(Bothering you again and again; always annoying.)

Example: The grownups sent the children out to play so that the children wouldn't be in their hair while they were talking.

In mint condition

(In excellent condition, as good as new.)

Example: My uncle's Erskine automobile, which was built in 1929, is in mint condition.

In earnest

(Seriously; in a determined way.)

Example: Bill did his homework in earnest.

(Often used like a predicate adjective. Sometimes used with dead, for emphasis.)

Example: Betty's friends thought she was joking when she said she wanted to be a doctor but she was in dead earnest.

In cold blood

(Without feeling or pity; in a purposely cruel way; coolly and deliberately.) This expression is usually used when talking about murder.

Example: The bank tellers were all shot and killed. The bank robbers murdered them all in cold blood.

A person can also be *cold blooded.*

Example: Only a cold-blooded killer could have killed those people.

In a good frame of mind

(In a happy mood.)

Example: After a long holiday and some much needed rest, Jim was in a good frame of mind when he went back to work.

A similar expression is *in a good mood.*

Example: The boss sure seems to be in a good mood this morning. He must have gotten some rest over the weekend.

One can also be *in a bad frame of mind*, or *in a bad mood*.

In a circle or in circles

(Without any progress; without getting anywhere; uselessly.)

Example: I have been working all day, yet, I haven't accomplished anything. It's as if I'm just going in circles.

Ill-gotten gains

(Goods or money obtained in an illegal or immoral fashion.)

Example: The jailed criminal had plenty of time to think about his ill-gotten gains.

Apple of one's eye

(Something or someone that is adored or cherished.)

Example: Vaishali has always been the apple of her father's eye.

Idiot box

(A television set.)

Example: Stop being lazy. You've done nothing but sit and watch that idiot box all afternoon.

In one's blood

(to be part of one's character or personality.)

Example: Don't trust Jason. It's in his blood to lie, and he'll never change.

Similar expressions include *in the blood* and *in one's genes*.

Hold on

(To wait, to pause or stop what you are doing momentarily.)

Usually used as a polite command. Often, but not always, followed by a time expression.

Example: Could you hold on for just a minute? I'd like to ask you a question before you continue with the lecture.

Have your cake and eat it too

(To enjoy two opposite advantages.)

Example: "I want that new dress," Mary complained, "but I don't want to spend that much money for it."

"You can't have your cake and eat it too," Mary's friend answered. "Either keep your money or buy the dress."

Horse sense

(A good understanding about what to do in life; good judgment; wisdom in making decisions.)

Example: Maybe George didn't go to college, but he has good horse sense.

Have cold feet

(To be afraid to do something.)

Example: Margie says she wants to get married someday, but we all know she probably won't. When it comes to marriage, she has cold feet.

You can also *get cold feet*.

Example: Barbie was supposed to get married yesterday, but she got cold feet and backed out at the last minute.

A similar expression is *to be chicken*.

Example: You won't go bungie jumping. You're too chicken.

Half a loaf is better than none

(To get part of what we want is better than getting nothing.)

Example: I wanted Rs. 5,000 for the work I did, but they only paid me Rs. 1,500. I guess half a loaf is better than nothing, though.

Have a heart of gold

(Have a kind and generous character)

Example: My teacher went out of his way to help me prepare for the test. He really has a heart of gold.

A similar expression is *to be big hearted* and to *have a big heart*.

Hair stand on end

(The hair on your head rises stiffly upwards as a result of fear or horror.)

Example: Tim's hair stood on end when he saw a ghost standing at the foot of his bed.

Similar expressions include *blood run cold* and *heart stand still*.

Example: Tim's blood ran cold when he saw a ghost standing at the foot of his bed.

To give off

(To release, emit, or produce a bad smell.)

Example: People who smoke give off a terrible smell.

Example: The paper plant on the outskirts of town gives off a terrible stink.

To give up

(To stop doing something, i.e. to give up a bad habit to stop trying.)

Example: If you would give up smoking you would not get sick so easily.

Example: I give up. I can't get this program to work. Why don't you try for a while?

Give in

(To agree to something that you first did not agree to.)

Example: At first, Bob didn't want to buy a new car because of the price. He eventually gave in, though, and now he is driving around in a brand new car.

Get rid of something

(To throw away; to dispose of)

Example: We got rid of all our old furniture when we moved to our new house.

Opposite expression: *hang on to something; to keep something.*

Example: Even though I have my favourite music on CDs, I want to hang on to my old record albums for posterity.

Get in touch with someone

(To contact someone by either phone, fax, or email.)

Example: I'll get in touch with you as soon as I get in town.

Similar expressions in include *touch base with* and *be in touch.*

Get a dose of one's own medicine

(To get the same bad treatment you give other people)

Example: Mark never helps out around the office, so it is no wonder no-one will help him with his new project. He is finally getting a dose of his own medicine.

Fall head over heels in love

(To fall deeply in love with someone. Usually used to describe how you feel after meeting someone for the first time.)

Example: Bashkim fell head over heels for Robin as soon as he saw her walk into the room.

You can also be *head over heals in love.*

Example: I am so envious of Mark and Sally. Even after five years of marriage they are still head over heels in love with each other.

Hand in

(To give something that is due to someone.)

Example: Please, hand in your homework when as you leave class.

Example: Please, hand your quiz in before you go home.

Hang by a thread

(To depend on a very small thing; be in doubt.)

Example: For three days Tom was so sick that his life hung by a thread.

Example: As Joe got ready to kick a field goal, he realised that the result of the game hung by a hair.

Handwriting on the wall

(A sign that something bad will happen.)

Example: Jim could read the handwriting on the wall as his employer had less and less work for him, so Jim began looking for another job.

Hand-to-mouth

(Not providing for the future; living from day to day; not saving for later.)

Example: John lives from hand-to-mouth, never saving any money. I wonder if he has given any thought to his future.

Half-hearted

(Lacking enthusiasm.)

Example: Jill went through the motions of learning Japanese while in class, but the teacher knew that Jill's efforts were only half-hearted.

Knock it off

(To stop talking about something considered not appropriate or nonsensical by the listener. Used frequently as an imperative. A sound meaning is to cease doing something; to quit. Heavily favoured in the imperative.)

Example: Come on, Joe, knock it off. You aren't making any sense at all.

Example: Come on boys, knock it off! You're going to break something if you don't stop hovering around.

Kindred spirits

(People who resemble each other in numerous ways, including their ways of thinking and feeling.)

Example: They are kindred spirits; they both like to go on long walks in the forest.

Kiss someone or something goodbye

(To lose or give up someone or something forever.)

Example: "If you won't marry Jane," Peter said to Tom, "you might as well kiss her goodbye because she'll be gone for good."

Keep one at a distance

[To avoid (someone's) company; not become too friendly toward someone.]

Example: Mr Smith is kind to the workers in his store but after work he keeps them at a distance.

Example: Beth likes Bill and is trying to be friendly, but he keeps her at arm's length.

Grow up

(To become adult in mind or judgment; become old enough to think or decide in important matters. Used to tell people to stop acting childish.)

Example: Pat wants to be a teacher when he grows up.

Example: Grow up, you're not a baby any more!

Grow out of

(To outgrow; become too mature for. To result from; arise.)

Example: As a child he had a habit of scratching his chin all the time; but he grew out of it.

Example: Tom's illness grew out of his tendency to overwork and neglect his health.

Grow on

(To become more interesting to or liked by.)

Example: At first Jim didn't like Mai Ling, but the more he saw of her the more she grew on him. Now they're best friends.

Get off easy

(To receive a lesser punishment than one deserves.)

Example: Jed could have gotten up to 5 years in prison. Instead he got off easy with only probation and a suspended sentence.

Get off cheap

(To pay less than the normal or expected price for something.)

Example: If you only paid Rs. 3,000 to have your car repaired, you got off cheap. I would have expected to pay at least Rs. 5,000.

Get lost

(Used as a command to tell someone to go away or to quit bothering you.)

Example: "Get lost! I want I study," John told Bert.

Green with envy

(Very jealous or envious of another person.)

Example: Alice's girlfriends were all green with envy when they saw her new engagement ring.

Green around the gills

(Pale-faced from fear or sickness; have sickly; nauseated.)

Example: Bobby looked a little green around the gills when he got off the roller coaster at the amusement park.

Grass is always greener

(We are often not satisfied and want to be somewhere else; a place that is far away or different seems better than where we are.)

Example: John is always changing his job because the grass always looks greener to him on the other side of the fence.

Grease one's palm

(To pay a person for something done or given especially dishonestly; bribe. Also, to give a tip; pay for a special favour or extra help.)

Example: Some politicians will help you if you grease their palms.

Example: We had to grease the palm of the waiter to get a table in the crowded restaurant.

Go steady

(To go on dates with the same person all the time; date just one person.)

Example: Tom and Martha have been going steady for about five years, but I heard they had a fight and broke up last week.

Draw a blank

(To try but fail to remember something or someone.)

Example: Randy tried to remember the new student's name but kept drawing a blank.

Keep pace

(To go as fast or at the same rate as another person or group; to not get behind.)

Example: When they go for a walk, Johnny has to take long steps to keep pace with his father.

Example: When Billy was moved to a more advanced class, he had to work hard to keep pace.

Keep in touch with

(To remain in communication with; maintain contact with.)

Example: Why didn't you keep in touch while you were in Europe! You could have at least emailed once in a while.

Keep one's chin up

(To be brave, be determined; face trouble with courage.)

Example: "Keep your chin up." Sally said to Jim when he found out he failed his exam. You'll do better next time."

Keep (one) posted

(To receive current information; to keep up to date.)

Example: My associates phoned me every day and kept me posted on new developments in our business.

Example: I'll keep you posted and let you know if things change.

Face the music

(To accept punishment for something you did wrong.)

Example: Jim was afraid to go home because he knew he would have to face the music for crashing his father's car.

Fall for

(To begin to like someone very much. To begin to love someone.)

Example: Jack knew by looking in her eyes that Jill had fallen for him.

Frown upon

(To look with disfavour upon someone or something. To not like something or someone.)

Example: Betty's father frowned upon her engagement to Mike. He didn't think Mike was good enough for his daughter.

Keep company

(To stay or go along with (someone) so that he/she will not be lonely. To go places together as a couple; to date just one person.)

Example: John kept Andy company while his parents went to the movies.

Example: Jim and Mary have been keeping company for over a year now.

Keep an eye on

(To watch carefully; not stop paying attention to. To watch and do what is needed for; mind.)

Example: A good driver keeps his eye on the road.

Example: Please, keep an eye on the baby while I run to the store.

Keep abreast (of)
(To be informed of the latest developments.)

Example: It is difficult to keep abreast of all the changes in technology in today's world.

Kangaroo court
(A self-appointed group that decides what to do to someone who is supposed to have done wrong.)

Example: The Chicago mob held a kangaroo court and shot the gangster who competed with Al Capone.

Jump to a conclusion
(To decide too quickly or without thinking or finding the facts.)

Example: When the police saw the knife in Mary's hand, they jumped to the conclusion that she was about to stab someone.

Just in case
(For an emergency; in order to be protected.)

Example: "Here are my car keys, Craig," Tom said. "My car should be okay where it is, but you should have them just in case you need to move it."

Just about
(Nearly; almost; practically.)

Example: Just about everyone in town came to hear the mayor speak.

Example: The dress came down to just about the middle of her knee.

Example: Has Mary finished peeling the potatoes? Just about.

From the bottom of one's heart

(With great feeling and sincerity; with great appreciation.)

Example: A mother loves her children from the bottom of her heart.

From scratch

(To start with nothing; to build something without any help from anything done before; to do something from the beginning.)

Example: "I hope you like this," Bob said as he handed the course outline to the dean. "I designed this course from scratch."

From rags to riches

(Suddenly making a lot of money. To become rich as if overnight.)

Example: Jim and Mary went from rags to riches when they won last months lottery.

Four eyes

(A person who wears glasses. A rude expression.)

Example: Fred hated wearing glasses because all the kids at school called him four eyes.

Couch potato

(A person who enjoys sitting on the couch watching TV all day.)

Example: Kim wanted nothing more than to be a couch potato all weekend, after working so hard all week.

Cat got one's tongue

(Not able or willing to talk because of shyness.)

Example: The little girl wouldn't talk so the teacher asked her if the cat had got her tongue.

Bite off more than one can chew

(To try to do more than you are able. To be over confident of one's ability.)

Example: He bit off more than he could chew when he accepted that extra assignment.

Be itching too

(To have a strong desire to do something.)

Example: Judy is itching to go to the nightclub tonight.

Be game

(To be willing to do something.)

Example: Are you game for a movie?

Sure, let's go.

Beat one's gums

(To engage in idle or meaningless talk. To talk too much.)

Example: I wish the speaker would stop beating his gums and get to the point.

At death's door

(Very near death)

Example: The Prime Minister was at death's door after suffering a serious stroke.

Back on one's feet

(Physically healthy again)

Example: My mother is back on her feet again after being sick with the flu for two weeks.

Black out
(Lose consciousness: faint)

Example: The football player blacked out after being hit by the other player.

Break out
(Begin showing a rash or other skin disorder)

Example: I broke out in a terrible rash after eating the raw shrimp at the restaurant.

Breathe one's last
(To die)

Example: The man finally breathed his last after a long illness.

Bring around/round
(Bring around/round- restore to health or consciousness, cure)

Example: The medical workers were able to bring the man around after the accident.

Bring to
(Restore to consciousness, wake from sleep/anaesthesia/hypnosis/fainting etc.)

Example: The woman was brought to soon after the car accident.

Catch a cold
(Get a cold)

Example: I caught a bad cold last week and had to miss three weeks of work.

Catch one's death of cold

[Become very ill (with a cold, flu, etc.)]

Example: The little boy was told to be careful in the rain or he would catch his death of cold.

Check-up

(A periodic inspection of a patient by a doctor)

Example: I went to have my annual check-up last week.

Clean bill of health

(A report or certificate that a person or animal is healthy)

Example: The doctor gave me a clean bill of health when I visited him last month.

Come down with

(Become sick with, catch)

Example: My niece came down with a bad cold and was unable to visit me last week.

Couch doctor

(A psychoanalyst who puts his patients on a couch)

Example: He was sent to see a couch doctor after his continued problems at work.

Draw blood

(Make someone bleed, get blood from someone)

Example: The doctor decided to draw some blood from the patient to check up on his blood sugar level.

Fall ill

(Become sick or ill)

Example: The man fell ill last winter and has not recovered yet.

Feel on top of the world

(Feel very healthy)

Example: I have been feeling on top of the world since I quit my job.

Flare up

[To begin again suddenly (illness etc.)]

Example: My mother's skin problems flared up when she started to use the new laundry soap.

Go under the knife

(Be operated on in surgery)

Example: His wife went under the knife at the hospital last evening.

Hang out one's shingle

(Give public notice of the opening of a doctor's office, etc,)

Example: The doctor decided to hang up his shingle as soon as he finished medical school.

Have a physical (examination)

(Get a medical check-up)

Example: Our company sent all the employees to have a physical last week.

Head shrinker

(A psychiatrist)

Example: The man was told to go and see a head shrinker after he threatened the woman in the store several times.

Just what the doctor ordered

(Exactly what is needed or wanted)

Example: A nice hot bath was just what the doctor ordered.

Look the picture of health

(Be in good health)

Example: My uncle was looking the picture of health when I saw him last week.

On the mend

(Healing, becoming better)

Example: My grandfather is on the mend after he broke his leg last week.

Out cold

(Unconscious, in a faint)

Example: As soon as the patient entered the operating room he was out cold because of the anaesthesia.

Over the worst

(Recovering from an illness)

Example: My brother is over the worst since his skiing accident last month.

Pull through

(Recover from a serious illness)

Example: The car accident was very bad and I don't think that the driver will pull through.

Run a temperature

(Have a higher than normal body temperature)

Example: The little boy is running a temperature and should stay in bed all day.

Run down

(Get into poor condition)

Example: He was working very hard last month and has become very run down.

Run some tests

(A doctor does some medical tests on a patient)

Example: The doctor has decided to run some tests on the patient.

Splitting headache

(A severe headache)

Example: I have been suffering from a splitting headache all morning.

Take a turn for the worse

(Become sicker)

Example: My aunt took a turn for the worse last week and is still in the hospital.

Take someone's temperature

(Measure someone's body temperature)

Example: The nurse took my temperature when I went to the hospital yesterday.

Throw up

(Vomit)

Example: The woman threw up several times after eating the bad shellfish.

Under the weather

(Not feeling well)

Example: My boss has been feeling under the weather all week and has not come to work during that time.

Back to the salt mines

(Back to work, humorous expression to express going back to unpleasant work)

Example: Well, lunch is over so let's go back to the salt mines for the afternoon.

Bad egg

(A bad person, bum)

Example: That man is a bad egg so you should try and avoid him if you can.

Big cheese

(An important person, a leader)

Example: He is a big cheese in his company so you should be very nice to him.

Bread and butter

(Basic needs of life (food, shelter, clothing)

Example: The voters are worried about bread and butter issues like jobs and taxes.

Bring home the bacon

(Earn your family's living)

Example: Recently he has been working very hard trying to bring home the bacon. He has no time to do anything else.

Butter up

(Flatter someone to try to get their favor or friendship)

Example: He spends most of his free time trying to butter up his boss so that he won't have to work so hard.

Carrot and stick

(Promising to reward or punish someone at the same time)

Example: The government took a carrot and stick approach to the people who were illegally protesting against the construction of the dam.

Chew the fat

(Chat)

Example: We stayed up very late last night chewing the fat about our university days.

Coffee break

(A break from work to rest and drink coffee)

Example: We usually take a 15-minute coffee break every morning about 10 o'clock.

Cool as a cucumber

(Calm, not nervous or anxious)

Example: He is always as cool as a cucumber and never worries about anything.

Cream of the crop

(Best of a group, the top choice)

Example: The company is well-known as a good place to work and is always able to hire the cream of the crop of university graduates.

Cry over spilt milk

(Cry or complain about something that has already happened)

Example: Don't cry over spilt milk. The past is past and you can't do anything to change it.

Cup of tea

(Something one enjoys or does well)

Example: Going to art galleries is not my cup of tea, so I think that I will stay home this evening and not go with you.

Cut the mustard

(Succeed, do well enough what needs to be done)

Example: He wasn't able to cut the mustard so he had to leave the army after only one year.

Duck soup

(A task that doesn't require much effort)

Example: It was duck soup. I was able to finish everything early last night.

Eat crow

(Admit one is mistaken or defeated, take back a mistaken statement)

Example: I was forced to eat crow and had to apologise for the mistake that I made about the restructuring of our company.

Eat dirt

(Accept another's insult or bad treatment)

Example: We made him eat dirt after he accused us of lying about the salary cut.

Eat humble pie

(Be humbled, admit one's error and apologize)

Example: Our boss was forced to eat humble pie after everyone realised that he had made the wrong budget estimate for next year.

Eat one's words

(Take back something one has said, admit something is not true)

Example: I told my boss that I would be leaving but later I had to eat my words and tell him that I wanted to stay.

Egg on

(Urge someone on)

Example: Many people at the soccer game were egged on by the drunken fans.

Finger in the pie

(Participate in something that is happening)

Example: He always tries to keep his finger in the pie so that he can control everything.

CHAPTER 6

Reading for Improving English

Though listening, speaking and writing are quite crucial while learning a language with the aim of improving conversation, reading too, may be quite helpful. There are many advantages associated with reading. Have a look at some of them.

Building a good vocabulary

Usually you will come across new words when you read. However, if you feel that you have come across too many new words, then you should try to read something simpler. But, if there are, say, a maximum of five new words per page, you will learn this vocabulary easily. You may not even need to use a dictionary because you can guess the meaning from the rest of the text (from the context). Thus, you would be able to learn how words are used in specific contexts. Obviously, it offers a double advantage. Not only your vocabulary would increase, but you would also learn how to put this vocabulary to use.

Getting examples for writing

When you read, you come across a number of examples for writing, such as how to narrate a story, how to present the climax in a novel, how to compose a speech, how to present statistics, how to write an essay, etc. Texts that you read show you structures and expressions that you can use when you write.

Getting to read English with proper grammatical structure

Most would agree that while writing, all try to use grammatically correct English whereas while talking, people usually express themselves by means of slang. So, by reading accurately written English, you would get to learn how to use grammatically correct English.

Read at your own speed

You can read at a pace you are comfortable with. You can read 4 pages in 20 minutes, or take half an hour to explore just one page. It doesn't matter. The choice is yours. You cannot easily do this when speaking or listening. This is one of the big advantages of reading because different people work at different speeds. It is here that reading scores an edge over speaking or listening.

Choose to read a topic of your interest

If you choose a topic of your interest to read, you would enjoy reading it. For example, if you like to read about football in your own language, why not read about football in English? You will get information about football and improve your English at the same time.

A few tips for reading

- Try to read something that you find easier to understand. If you need to stop every three words to look in a dictionary, it is not interesting for you and you will soon be discouraged. So, read something that improves your English, thereby adding to your confidence.

- Make a note of every new word you come across. If there are four or five new words on a page, write them in your vocabulary book. But you don't have to write them while you read. Instead, try to guess their meaning as you read;

mark them with a pen; then come back when you have finished reading to check in a dictionary and add them to your vocabulary book. It would certainly enhance your vocabulary.

- Make it a regular practice to read. For example, read for a short time once a day. Fifteen minutes every day is better than two hours every Sunday. Fix a time to read and keep to it. For example, you could read for fifteen minutes when you go to bed, or when you get up, or at lunchtime. But keep in mind, it should be a regular practice.

- Be organised. Always have with yourself:
  - something to read
  - a marker to highlight difficult words
  - a dictionary
  - your vocabulary book
  - a pen to write down the new words

- Read something that is of some interest to you. You may choose a magazine or a book etc. about a subject that you enjoy reading about.

What to read?

Newspapers

English newspapers are easily available all over the world these days. They are interesting to read because they are about real life and the news. But they are not easy to read. Try reading newspapers if your level is intermediate or above. It is bound to increase not only your knowledge of the world but also of the language.

Magazines

A number of monthly, fortnightly and even weekly magazines are available these days. You can find English-language magazines in many large cities around the world. If you cannot find the magazine you want in your town, you may be able to order it for delivery. Many magazines have pictures, which can help your understanding. You will need an intermediate level for most magazines, but a pre-intermediate level may be ok for some magazines. There are several magazines for people belonging to different age groups such as magazines for children, teenaged people and adults. So you may choose one according to your age group.

Moreover, there are magazines on every subject as listed below (you may choose a magazine based on the subject that interests you):

- Politics
- Sports
- Cars
- Music
- Romance
- Travel
- Language
- Fashion

Books

Books can be divided mainly into:

- Non-fiction (history, biography, travel, cooking etc.)
- Fiction (stories and novels)

Though there are a number of books to choose from, you may find that some are easier to read than others. It often depends on the author. Agatha Christie, for example, wrote in an easier style and with simpler vocabulary than Stephen King. You can buy books in specialised English-language bookshops in large cities around the world. You may also be able to find some English-language books in libraries. And, if you have a British Council in your city, you can borrow many English-language books from their library. British Council Library is not the only one, there are many others in the cities. If you are a student, you may explore your school/college/university library as well.

Short stories

In case you get bored with bulky books, short stories can be a good choice when learning a language because they are short. It's like reading a whole book in a few pages. You have all the excitement of a story in a book, but you only have to read 5,000 or 10,000 words. So you can quite quickly finish the story and feel that you have achieved something. Short stories are published in magazines, in books of short stories, and on the Internet. You can choose any of these to read short stories.

Readers

You may choose readers too. These are books that are specially published to be easy to read. They are short and with simple vocabulary. They are usually available at different levels, so you should be able to find the right level for you. Many readers are stories by famous authors in simple form. This is an excellent way for you to start practising reading. Not only would it be an easier, but an interesting way too.

Cornflakes Packets

'Cornflakes Packets', denote any product you can buy that has English writing on or with it. If you buy a box of chocolates, or a new camera, why not read the description or instructions in English? There are many such examples, and they all give you an opportunity to read real English:

- Airline tickets
- Cans or packets of food

- Bottles of drink
- Tapes and CDs
- User guides for videos, computers...etc.

Poetry

In case you enjoy reading poetry, try reading some English-language poems. They may not be easy to understand because of the style and vocabulary. But, if you work at it, you can usually get an idea – or a feeling – of what the poet is trying to say. Remember if you make a genuine attempt, reading poetry may be fun.

Chapter 7

Effective Presentations

Public speaking

Good public speaking certainly denotes good communication skills. Many people feel anxious about giving a formal talk or presentation in public. The main reasons why so many people feel anxious in this situation appear to be:

- **Unfamiliar Situation:** Since most people speak formally only rarely to an audience, the novelty of the situation is a cause of apprehension.

- **Lack of Confidence:** This stems often from a feeling that others are better speakers than ourselves, or that they know more about the topic in question.

- **Sense of Isolation:** The speaker is alone, the centre of attraction – and vulnerable.

- **Self-Consciousness:** Most of the speakers shiver when they think about their accents, grammar, voice and image generally.

- **Fear of looking Foolish:** We may worry that we will forget what we wanted to say, and will stumble over our words, will say the 'wrong' thing, etc.

- **Fear of the Consequences:** For example, being 'judged' by others, particularly tutors, as lacking in ability or insight because of a poor public presentation.

How 'nerves' affect you physically?

The signs of anxiety are all too painfully familiar to those affected. They include increased heart and breathing rates, increased adrenaline, over-rapid reactions, and a tension in the shoulder and neck area. These bodily changes can affect the voice, making it sound tremulous, or disjointed by over-rapid breathing.

Some of the fear experienced when we have to speak in public can be overcome by following the three Ps: Planning, Preparation, Practise. Time spent on these activities means that you are really thinking through the whole process, from what to say, to how to say it. Being prepared is half the battle to overcoming anxiety.

Planning

- This involves setting your objectives, considering the purpose of your presentation and the message you are trying to get across to your audience.

- Know your audience. Consider these question: How many will you be speaking to? Why will they be there? What is their prior knowledge? What are their expectations?

- Brainstorm to get your ideas down on paper and then select and order the points you want to make.

- Consider the time you have been allotted and how much you can reasonably say in that time.

- Decide how you are going to structure your presentation. Basically, you need an introduction, a middle and a conclusion. This is often referred to as, 'Tell them what you're going to tell them; tell them; then tell them again.'

- The first four minutes are the time when you are likely to have the attention of your audience, it is important to make an impact with your introduction.

- Make your notes. Unless you are reading a speech/paper, your notes should consist of key words and phrases which should be just enough to jog your memory and remind you of points you want to make. You can use cue cards, mind maps or ordinary notes on paper depending on your preference, but make them stand out.

Preparation

- Prepare any visual aids you want to use. These can be transparencies for an overhead projector (OHP), slides, flip chart or black/white board etc.

- Make sure any equipment you need is available and that you are familiar with it.

- Check your venue and familiarise yourself with it if possible.

Practise

- Practise your presentation out loud, either on your own or in front of friends who will give you helpful feedback.

- Use a tape recorder so you can listen to yourself. This will identify:

  - How much you vary the tone of your voice?

  - Any points you might want to emphasise.

  - The amount of enthusiasm you communicate.

- You could practice in front of a mirror to identify any mannerisms or gestures you might want to change. Not everyone advocates doing this, for the simple reason that you will be giving your talk to other people not to yourself.

- Practise smiling. By smiling you are conveying the message that you are pleased to be speaking to your audience. This makes them feel more comfortable, which in turn affects how you relate to your audience.

Few tips for public speakers

No matter how much you doubt your own speaking abilities, you will be amazed at how these tips and techniques will help you make effective presentations in any situation – from one-on-one to large groups!

To quote Sir Winston Churchill, "Some people are born public speakers, some people achieve public speaking and some people have public speaking thrust upon them."

Whatever your situation or circumstances, Speak For Yourself. This may help.

Unstoppable confidence is the unshakable belief in yourself and what you are capable of. What separates the people who achieve their dreams and the people who languish is confidence. With confidence, people pursue their goals and persevere until they achieve them. Without confidence, time passes, as the people stay stuck in their rigid comfort zones, unable to escape.

- Dealing with fear:
    - Shake some of the tension out of your body, before presenting, and take three deep breaths.
    - Give yourself positive messages: My speech is a gift to the audience. I have something valuable to say and they want to hear it.
    - Be organised and practice.
- Considering your audience:
    - Welcome them.
    - Be loud enough.
    - Explain your terms. Put difficult words on overheads.
    - Keep in mind that people learn differently. Some people understand visuals better than others. Some people are hard of hearing.
- Expression and enthusiasm:
    - Communicate your interest in the topic. You can make topics more interesting by making them interactive.

- Communicate interest with sincerity, eye contact and energy.
- Starting your speech:
  - Begin with a question to get them thinking about your topic.
  - Engage those who have an answer to that question.
- Using posture and gestures:
  - Bring the microphone up to your chin. Do not lean into the microphone.
  - Gesture can emphasise your points and show enthusiasm.
  - Stand upright or move purposefully into the audience. Shuffling distracts the audience from your message.
- Making eye contact:
  - Try and look at everyone so they feel included.
- Using audio/visual:
  - Make sure your equipment is working before your presentation.
  - Move to the screen when possible. Standing in front of the overhead projector often blocks the screen.
  - Point to features on your visuals, so that everyone in the audience can follow.

CHAPTER 8

Telephonic Conversation

Conversation can be face to face or over the telephone. Where face to face conversation and public speaking demand confidence on the part of the speaker, telephonic conversation too needs certain rules to be followed:

1. **Speak slowly and clearly**

   Listening to someone speaking in a second language over the telephone can be very challenging because you cannot see the person you are trying to hear. However, it may be even more difficult for the person you are talking with to understand you. You may not realise that your pronunciation is not clear because your teacher, fellow students or friends know and understand you. Pay special attention to your weak areas (such as r's and l's or b's and v's) when you are on the phone. If you are nervous about using the phone in English, you may notice yourself speaking very quickly. Practise or write down what you are going to say and take a few deep breaths before you make a phone call.

2. **Make sure you understand the other speaker**

   Do not pretend to understand everything you hear over the telephone. Even native speakers ask each other to repeat and confirm information from time to time. This is especially important if you are taking a message for someone else. Learn the appropriate expressions that English speakers use when they do not hear something properly. Do not be afraid to remind the person to slow down more than once. Keep your telephone in an area that is away from other noise distractions such as a radio or television.

3. **Practise with a friend**

Ask another person to practise talking on the phone with you. You might choose one night a week and take turns phoning each other at a certain time. Try to talk for at least fifteen minutes. You can talk socially, or role play different scenarios in a business environment. If you do not have access to a telephone, you can practise by setting two chairs up back to back. The most important thing about practising telephone English is that you aren't able to see each other's mouths. It is amazing how much people lip-read without realising.

4. **Use recordings**

There are many ways to get free telephone English practice. After business hours, you can call and listen to recorded messages. Write down what you hear the first time, and then call back and check if your notes are accurate. Use the phone in your everyday life. Call for a pizza delivery instead of going out to eat. Call a salon to book a hair appointment. You can even phone the movie theatre to ask for the listings instead of using the newspaper. Some large cities have free recordings you can call for information such as your daily horoscope or the weather. Make sure that you are not going to get charged for these numbers first. Some products have free phone numbers on the packaging that you can call for information. Think of a question you might want to ask and call the free number! For example, call the number on the back of the cereal box and ask for coupons. You will have to give your name and address. Make sure you have a pen handy so that you can repeat the information and check your comprehension.

5. **Learn telephone etiquette (manners)**

    The way that you speak to your best friend on the phone is very different to the way you should speak to someone in a business setting. Many speakers make the mistake of being too direct on the telephone. It is possible that the person on the other line will think that you are being rude on purpose if you do not use formal language in certain situations. Sometimes just one word such as 'could' or 'may' is necessary in order to sound polite. You should use the same modals you would use in a formal 'face-to-face' situation. Take time to learn how to answer the phone and say goodbye in a polite manner, as well as all the various ways one can start and end a conversation casually.

6. **Practise dates and numbers**

    It only takes a short time to memorise English Phonetic Spelling, but it is something that you will be able to use in any country. You should also practise saying dates and numbers aloud. You and a friend can write out a list of dates and numbers and take turns reading them over the phone to each other. Record what you hear. Swap papers the next day and check your answers.

Telephone language

Here are some typical phrases that you can use in a telephone conversation:

Answering the phone

*   Hello? (Informal)
*   Thank you for calling Boyz Autobody. Jody speaking. How can I help you?
*   Doctor's office.

Introducing yourself

*   Hey Kunal. It's Sarika calling. (Informal)

- Hello, this is Rashmi Mehta calling.
- Hi, it's Amit from the dentist's office here.

Asking to speak with someone

- Is Kunal in? (Informal)
- Is Jatin there, please? (Informal)
- Can I talk to your sister? (Informal)
- May I speak with Mr. Kishan, please?
- Would the doctor be in/available?

Connecting someone

- Just a sec. I'll get him. (Informal)
- Hang on one second. (Informal)
- Please hold and I'll put you through to his office.
- One moment please.
- All of our operators are busy at this time. Please hold for the next available person.

Making special requests

- Could you please repeat that?
- Would you mind spelling that for me?
- Could you speak up a little please?
- Can you speak a little slower, please. My English isn't very strong.
- Can you call me back? I think we have a bad connection.
- Can you please hold for a minute? I have another call.

Taking a message for someone

- Tanu's not in. Who's this? (Informal)
- I'm sorry, Lisa's not here at the moment. Can I ask who's calling?

- I'm afraid he's stepped out. Would you like to leave a message?
- He's on lunch right now. Who's calling please?
- He's busy right now. Can you call again later?
- I'll let him know you called.
- I'll make sure she gets the message.

Leaving a message with someone

- Yes, can you tell him his wife called, please.
- No, that's okay; I'll call back later.
- Yes, it's Yogita from CompInc. here. When do you expect her back in the office?
- Thanks, could you ask him to call Bela when he gets in?
- Do you have a pen handy? I do not think he has my number.
- Thanks. My number is 222-3456, extension 12.

Confirming information

- Okay, I've got it all down.
- Let me repeat that just to make sure.
- Did you say 555 Palki Street?
- You said your name was Tarun, right?
- I'll make sure he gets the message.

Listening to an answering machine

- Hello. You've reached 222-6789. Please leave a detailed message after the beep. Thank you.
- Hi, this is Tina. I'm sorry I'm not available to take your call at this time. Leave me a message and I'll get back to you as soon as I can.
- Thank you for calling Dr. Modi's office. Our office hours are 9am-5pm, Monday-Friday. Please call back during these hours, or leave a message after the tone. If this is an

emergency please call the hospital at 222-7896.

Leaving a message on an answering machine

- Hey Mikako. It's Yuka. Call me! (Informal)
- Hello, this is Radhika calling for Shweta. Could you please return my call as soon as possible? My number is 334-5689. Thank you.
- Hello Maxwell. This is Shruti from the doctor's office calling. I just wanted to let you know that you're due for a check-up this month. Please give us a ring/buzz whenever it's convenient.

Finishing a conversation

- Well, I guess I better get going. Talk to you soon.
- Thanks for calling. Bye for now.
- I have to let you go now.
- I have another call coming through. I better run.
- I'm afraid that's my other line.
- I'll talk to you again soon. Bye.

CHAPTER 9

Small Talk

In most English-speaking countries, it is normal and necessary to make 'small talk' in certain situations. Small talk is a casual form of conversation that 'breaks the ice' or fills an awkward silence between people. Even though you may feel shy using your second language, it is sometimes considered rude to say nothing. Just as there are certain times when small talk is appropriate, there are also certain topics that people often discuss during these moments. Thus, a small talk has a significance of its own.

Small Talk: Who, What, Where, When, Why?

Who makes small talk?

People in almost all the relationships use small talk. The most common type of people to use small talk is those who do not know each other at all. Though we often teach children not to talk to strangers, adults are expected to say at least a few words in certain situations. It is also common for people who are only acquaintances, often called a 'friend of a friend', to use small talk. Other people who have short casual conversations are office employees who may not be good friends but work in the same department. Customer service representatives, waitresses, hairdressers and receptionists often make small talk with customers. If you happen to be outside when the postman comes to your door you might make small talk with him too. It would at least enable you to overcome your hesitation and initiate a talk with others.

What do people make small talk about?

You can choose a topic of mutual interest for a small talk. There are certain 'safe' topics that people usually make small talk about. The weather is probably the number one thing that people who do not know each other well discuss. Sometimes even friends and family members discuss the weather when they meet or start a conversation. Another topic that is generally safe is current events. As long as you are not discussing a controversial issue, such as a recent law concerning equal rights, it is usually safe to discuss the news. Sports news is a very common topic, especially if a local team or player is in a tournament or play-off or doing extremely well or badly. Entertainment news, such as a celebrity who is in town, is another good topic. If there is something that you and the other speaker has in common, that may also be acceptable to talk about. For example, if the bus is extremely full and there are no seats available you might talk about reasons why. Similarly, people in an office might casually discuss the new paint or furniture.

Where do people make small talk?

A small talk can be made almost anywhere. People make small talk just about anywhere, but there are certain places where it is very common. Most often, small talk occurs in places where people are waiting for something. For example, you might chat with another person who is waiting for the bus to arrive, or to the person beside you waiting to get on an aeroplane. People also make small talk in a doctor or dentist's waiting room, or in queues at the grocery store. At the office, people make small talk in elevators or lunchrooms and even in restrooms, especially if there is a line-up. Some social events (such as a party) require small talk among guests who do not know each other very well. For example, you might talk to someone you do not know at the punch bowl, or at the poolside. It is called 'mingling' when people walk around in a social setting and talk to a variety of people.

Thus a small talk may even serve to introduce two strangers to each other.

When do people make small talk?

The most common time for small talk to occur is the first time you see or meet someone on a given day. For example, if you see a co-worker in the lounge you might say hello and discuss the sports or weather. However, the next time you see each other you might just smile and say nothing. If there is very little noise that might be an indication that it is the right time to initiate a casual conversation. You should only spark up a conversation after someone smiles and acknowledges you. Do not interrupt two people in order to discuss something unimportant such as the weather. If someone is reading a book or writing a letter at the bus stop, it is not appropriate to initiate a conversation either. Another good time to make small talk is during a break in a meeting or presentation when there is nothing important going on. Finally, it is important to recognise the cue when the other person wants the conversation to stop.

Why do people make small talk?

What could be the reason(s) behind a small talk? There are a few different reasons why people use small talk. The first, and most obvious, is to break an uncomfortable silence. Another reason, however, is simply to fill time. That is why it is so common to make small talk when you are waiting for something. Some people make small talk in order to be polite. You may not feel like chatting with anyone at a party, but it is rude to just sit in a corner by yourself. After someone introduces you to another person, you do not know anything about them, so in order to show a polite interest in getting to know them better, you have to start with some small talk.

CHAPTER 10

Conversation Principles

There can be no doubt that of all the accomplishments prized in modern society, the one of being agreeable in conversation is the very first. It may be called the social result of western civilization, beginning with the Greeks. Whatever contempt the North American Indian or the Mohammedan Tartar may feel for talking as mere chatter, it is agreed among us that people must meet frequently, both men and women, and that not only is it agreeable to talk, but that it is a matter of common courtesy to say something, even when there is hardly anything to say.

Every civilized man and woman feels, or ought to feel, this duty; it is the universal accomplishment which all must practise, and as those who fail signally to attain it are punished by the dislike or neglect of society, so those who succeed beyond the average receive a just reward, not only in the constant pleasure they reap from it, but in the esteem which they gain from their fellows. Many men and many women owe the whole of a great success in life to this and nothing else. An agreeable young woman will always carry away the palm in the long run from the most brilliant player or singer who has nothing to say. And though men are supposed to succeed in life by dead knowledge, or by acquaintance with business, it is often by their social qualities, by their agreeable way of putting things, and not by their more ponderous merits that they prevail. In the high profession of diplomacy, both home and foreign, this is pre-eminently the case.

But, quite apart from all these serious profits, and better than them all, is the daily pleasure derived from good conversation by those who can attain to it themselves or enjoy it in others. It is a perpetual intellectual feast, it is an ever-ready recreation, a deep and lasting comfort, costing no outlay but that of time, requiring no appointments but a small company, limited neither to any age nor any sex, the delight of prosperity, the solace of adversity, the eternal and essential expression of that social instinct which is one of the strongest and best features in human nature...

The old Greeks set it down as an axiom that a loud or harsh voice betokened bad breeding, and any one who hears the lower classes discussing any topic at the corners of the streets may notice not merely their coarseness and rudeness in expression, but also the loudness and harshness of their voices, in support of this observation. The habit of wrangling with people who will not listen without interruption, and who try to shout down their company, nay even the habit of losing one's temper, engenders a noisy and harsh way of speaking, which naturally causes a prejudice against the talker in good society. Even the dogmatic or over-confident temper which asserts opinions loudly, and looks round to command approval or challenge contradiction, chills good conversation by setting people against the speaker, whom they presume to be a social bully and wanting in sympathy.

Nothing attracts more at first hearing than a soft and sweet tone of voice. It generally suggests a deeper well of feeling than the speaker possesses, and certainly preju dices people as much in his favor as a grating or loud utterance repels them. It is to be classed with personal beauty, which disposes every one to favour the speaker, and listen to him or her with sympathy and attention. This sweetness in the tone of the voice is chiefly a natural gift, but it may also be improved, if not acquired, by constant and careful training in early years. It can certainly be marred by constant straining and shouting. It should therefore be carefully cultivated or protected in youth as a valuable vantage ground in social intercourse.

Similarly, the presence of a strong local accent, though there are cases where it gives raciness to wit and pungency to satire, is usually a hindrance in conversation, especially at its outset, and among strangers. It marks a man as provincial, and hence is akin to vulgarity and narrowness of mind. It suggests, too, that the speaker has not moved much about the world, or even in the best society of his native country, in which such provincialism is carefully avoided, and set down as an index of mind and manners below the highest level. Hence, all careful educators endeavour to eradicate peculiarities of accent or pronunciation in children, and justly, though we have all met great talkers whose Scotch burr or Irish brogue seemed an essential feature of their charm. If this be so, no education can eradicate it. In lesser people, to be provincial is distinctly an obstacle in the way, even though a great mind may turn it into a stepping-stone.

There is yet another almost physical disability or 'damage to conversation, which is akin to provincialism, and which consists in disagreeable tricks in conversation, such as the constant and meaningless repetition of catchwords and phrases, such as the unmeaning oaths of our grandfathers; such as inarticulate sounds of assent; such as contortions of the face, which so annoy the hearer by their very want of meaning and triviality as to excite quite a disproportionate dislike to the speaker, and to require great and sterling qualities to counterbalance it. However apt a man's internal furniture may be for conversation, he may make it useless by being externally disagreeable. How often when we praise a friend as a good talker do we hear the reply, "I should like him well enough if he did not worry me with his don't you know, or his what" or something else so childishly small, that we shudder to think how easily a man may forfeit his position or popularity among civilized men in their daily intercourse. But, modern society, which ought to be of all things in human life the most easy and unconstrained, is growing every day more tyrannical and only to be kept in good humour by careful attention to its unwritten behests, unless, indeed, we have the power to bend it to our will, and force it to follow our lead instead of driving us along like slaves.

The highest and best of all the moral conditions for conversation is what we call tact. It can be said a condition, for it is very doubtful whether it can be called a single and separate quality; more probably it is a combination of intellectual quickness with lively sympathy. But so clearly is it an intellectual quality, that of all others it can be greatly improved, if not actually acquired, by long experience in society. Like all social excellences it is almost given as a present to some people, while others with all possible labour never acquire it. As in billiard playing, shooting, cricket, and all these other facilities which are partly mental and partly physical, many never can pass a certain amount of mediocrity; but still, even those who have the talent must practise it, and only become really distinguished after hard work. So it is in art. Music and painting are not to be attained by the crowd. Not even the just criticism of these arts is attainable without certain natural gifts; but a great deal of practise in good galleries and at good concerts, and years spent among artists, will do much to make even moderately endowed people sound judges of excellence.

Tact, which is the sure and quick judgment of what is suitable and agreeable in society, is likewise one of those delicate and subtle qualities or a combination of qualities which is not very easily defined, and therefore not teachable by fixed precepts; but we can easily see that it is based on all the conditions we have already discussed. Some people attain it through sympathy; others through natural intelligence; others through a calm temper; others again by observing closely the mistakes of their neighbours.

As its name implies, it is a sensitive touch in social matters, which feels small changes of temperature, and so guesses at changes of temper; which sees the passing cloud on the expression of one face, or the eagerness of another that desires to bring out something personal for others to enjoy. This quality of tact is of course applicable far beyond mere actual conversation. In nothing is it more useful than in preparing the right conditions for a pleasant society, in choosing the people who will be in mutual sympathy, in thinking over pleasant subjects of talk and suggesting them, in seeing that all disturbing conditions are kept out, and that the members who are to converse should be all without those small inconveniences which damage society so vastly out of proportion to their intrinsic importance.

This social skill is generally supposed to be congenital, especially in some women, and no one thinks of laying down rules for it, as its application is so constant, various, and often sudden. Yet it is certain that any one may improve himself by reflection on the matter, and so avoid those shocking mistakes which arise from social stupidity. Thus, in the company of a woman who is a man's third wife, most people will instinctively avoid jokes or anecdotes of comparison between a man's several wives. But quite apart from instinct, an experienced man who is going to tell a story which may have too much point for some of those present, will look round and consider each member of the party, and if there be a single stranger there whose views are not familiar to him, he will forego the pleasure of telling the story rather than make the social mistake of hurting even one of the guests. On the other hand, this very example shows how a single stranger may spoil a whole conversation by inducing caution in the speakers and imposing upon them such reserve as is inconsistent with a perfectly easy flow of talk.

Another evidence of tact is the perception that a topic has been sufficiently discussed, and that it is on the point of becoming tedious. There is nothing which elderly people should watch more carefully in themselves, for even those once gay and brilliant are almost certain to become prosy with age, and to dwell upon their favorite topics as if this preference were shared by all society. But even the young must be here perpetually upon the watch, and show their tact by refraining from too many questions or too much argument upon any single subject, which becomes a bore to others. Every host and hostess should make it their first duty to watch this human weakness, and should lead away the conversation when it threatens to stay in the same groove. It is better to do this bluntly and confessedly than to refrain from doing it. But, the quality of tact, as it quickly perceives the growing mischief, is also quick of resource in devising such interruptions as may seem natural or unavoidable, so as to beguile the company into new paths, and even make the too persistent members lay aside their threadbare discussion without regret.

If wit be the quick flash, the electric spark, the play of summer lightning which warms the colour of conversation, humour is the sustained side of the ridiculous, the comic way of looking at things and people, which may be manifested either in comment upon the statements made by others or in narrating one's own experiences. Of course in receiving and commenting upon what is being said, no preparation is possible. It depends altogether upon a mental attitude, which looks out with a smile upon the world, and exposes the ridiculous side of human life not more by irony of comment than by mock approval of social vices, mock indignation at social virtues, seriousness when false comedy is being produced, raillery when false tragedy is being paraded with insincerity or empty bombast. In these and a hundred other ways humour receives and criticizes what other people say in a company; and if it be coupled with kindliness o f heart and with tact, may be regarded as the very highest of conversational virtues.

Analogous to this is the display of humour, not in receiving but in producing ideas in company. The humorist is the only good and effective story-teller; for if he is to monopolise a conversation, and require others to listen to him, it must be by presenting human life under a fresh and piquant aspect in fact, as a little comedy. Thus, the lifelike portrayal of any kind of foible-pomposity, obsequiousness, conceit, hypocrisy, nay even of provincial accent or ungrammatical language-ensures a pleased and therefore agreeable audience, and opens the way for easy and sympathetic intercourse. It is perhaps not too much to say that in any society where conventionality becomes a threatening power, humour is our great safeguard from this kind of vulgarity. The humourous exhibition of foibles is the most effective way we know of bringing them before the public mind, and of warning people that here is a judge whose censure is really to be feared.

Remember, a man who can say a good thing or make a person appear ridiculous may be so proud of his power that he exercises it at the cost of good taste and even of real humanity. The great wit is often cruel, and even glories in wounding to the quick the sensibilities of others. If he can carry some of the company with him he has a wicked enjoyment in making one of the rest a butt or target for his shafts, and so destroying all wholesome conversation. He may leave in the minds of his society an admiration of his talent, but often a serious dislike of his character. With such feelings abroad he will injure conversation far more than he promotes it. People may consent to go into his company to hear him talk, but will avoid talking in his presence.

The excesses of the humourist are, perhaps, rather those of a complacent selfishness, which does not hesitate to monopolise the company with long stories in which all do not feel an interest. But humour is its own antidote; and if a man has the true vein in him he will also have the tact to feel when he is tedious, and when his fun is out of harmony with his hearers. For these reasons, it is not only a higher but a safer gift than wit for the purpose of conversation; the pity of it is that so few possess it, and that there is hardly any use in trying to attain it by education. No doubt the constant society of an elder or superior who looks at things in this way may stimulate it in the young, but with the danger of making them sarcastic and satirical, which are grave faults, and which are the distortion of humour to ill-natured and unsocial purposes, so that even in this view of the matter education in humour may turn out a very mischievous failure.

On the whole, we must set ourselves to carry on society and to make good conversation without any large help from these brilliant but dangerous gifts. Occasional flashes will occur to ordinary people, and sometimes the very circumstances themselves will create a situation so humourous that it requires no genius to bring it home to the company. But beyond the necessary cautions above indicated, we cannot bring it into any systematic doctrine of social intercourse.

These last remarks are very applicable to the case next before us, when conversation is among a few-say from four to eight people-a form of society the best and most suitable for talk, but which is now rather the exception, from the common habit of crowding our rooms or our tables, and getting rid of social obligations as if they were commercial debts. Indeed, many of our young people have so seldom heard a general conversation that they grow up in the belief that their only duty in society will be to talk to one man or woman at a time. So serious are the results of the fashion of large dinner parties. For really good society, no dinner table should be too large to exclude general conversation, and no couples should sit together who are likely to lapse into private discourse.

It is generally thought the fault of the host or hostess if such an evening turns out a failure; and, indeed, it is possible to bring one incongruous person into a small company who will so chill or disturb the rest that conversation languishes. But this case is rare, and the fault usually lies with the company, none of whom take the trouble to tide over any difficulty, or seek to draw out from those present what they like or want to say.

In the very forefront there stares us in the face that very awkward period which even the gentle. As the worst possible for conversation, the short time during which people are assembling and waiting for the announcement of dinner. If the 'witty man were not usually a selfish person, who will not exhibit his talent without the reward of full and leisurely appreciation, this is the real moment to show his powers. A brilliant thing, said at the very start, which sets people laughing, and makes them forget that they are waiting, may alter the whole complexion of the party, may make the silent and distant people feel themselves drawn into the sympathy of common merriment, and thaw the iciness which so often fetters Anglo-Saxon society. But, as this faculty is not given to many, so the average man may content himself with having something ready to tell, and this, if possible, in answer to the usual questions expressed or implied: Is there any news this afternoon? There are few days that the daily papers will not afford to the intelligent critic something ridiculous, either in style or matter, which has escaped the ordinary public; some local event, nay, even some local tragedy, may suggest a topic not worth more than a few minutes of attention, which will secure the interest of minds vacant, and perhaps more hungry to be fed than their bodies. Here, then, if anywhere in the whole range of conversation, the man or woman who desires to be agreeable may venture to think beforehand, and bring with them something ready, merely as the first kick or starting point to make the evening run smoothly.

When the company has settled down to dinner, the first care should be to prevent it breaking into couples, and for that purpose some one opposite should be addressed or some question asked which may evoke answers from various people. Above all, however, the particular guest of the night, or the person best known as a wit or story teller, should not be pressed or challenged at the outset-a sort of vulgarity which makes him either shy or angry at being so manifestly exploit by the company, so that he is likely either to turn silent or say some ill-humoured things.

The main advice to be given to women to help them in making such a small company agreeable, is to study politics. A vast number of clever and well-read women exclude themselves from a large part of the serious talk of men by neglecting this engrossing and ever-fruitful topic of conversation. Literature, of course, is a still more various and interesting subject; but here, perhaps, the defect lies with men who are so devoted to practical life that they lose their taste for general reading. Except for politics, the daily papers seldom afford any literary food fit for good conversation.

The topic which ought to be common to both and always interesting, is the discussion of human character and human motives. If the novel be so popular a form of literature, how can the novel in real life fail to interest an intelligent company? People of serious temper and philosophic habit will be able to confine themselves to large ethical views, and the general dealings of men; but to average people, both men and women, and, perhaps most of all, to busy men who desire to find in society relaxation from their toil, that lighter and more personal kind of criticism on human affairs will prevail which is known as gossip.

This may, therefore, be the suitable moment to consider the place of gossip in the theory of conversation; for though gossip is not only possible but usual in the private discourse of two people, and possible, too, in a large society, its real home and natural exercising ground is the society of a few people intimate with the same surroundings.

It is usual for all people, especially those who most indulge in it, to censure gossip as a crime, as a violation of the Ninth

Commandment, as a proof of idleness and vain curiosity, as a frivolous waste of the time giver us for mental improvement. Yet the censure is seldom serious. These people cannot but feel obscurely what they are either afraid to speak out or have not duly considered, that the main object of conversation is neither instruction nor moral improvement but recreation. It is of course highly desirable that all our amusements should be both intellectually and morally profitable, and we may look back with special satisfaction upon any conversation which included these important objects. But the main and direct object is recreation, mental relaxation, happy idleness; and from this point of view it is improbable for any sound theory of conversation to ignore or depreciate gossip, which is, perhaps, the main factor in agreeable talk throughout society.

The most harmless form is the repeating of small details about personages great either in position or intellect, which give their empty names a personal colour, and so bring them nearer and more clearly into view. The man who has just come from the society of kings and queens, or great generals, or politicians, or literary men whose names are exceptionally prominent at the time, can generally furnish some personal details by which people imagine they can explain to themselves great and unexpected results. Who has not heard with interest such anecdotes about Mr. Gladstone, or Prince Bis marck, or Victor Emmanuel? And what book has ever acquired more deserved and lasting reputation than Boswell's Life of Johnson?

The latest development of the literary side of gossip is to be seen in what are called the society papers, which owe their circulation to their usefulness in furnishing topics for this kind of conversation. All the funny sketches of life and character are of the character of gossip, subtracting the mischievous element of personality; and though most people will think this latter an essential feature in our meaning when we talk of gossip, it is not so; it is the trivial and passing, the unproven and suspected, which is the main thing, for it is quite possible to bring any story under the notion while suppressing the names of the actors.

Next to the retailing of small personal points about great people comes the narrating of deeper interests belonging to small people, especially the affairs of the heart, which we pursue so assiduously even in feigned characters. But here it is that all the foibles of our neighbours come under survey, and that a great deal of calumny and slander may be launched upon the world by mere shrug and innuendo. The reader will remember with what effect this side of gossip is brought out in Sheridan's School for Scandal.

It is idle to deny that there is no kind of conversation more fascinating than this, but its immorality may easily become such as to shock honest minds, and the man who in dulges in it freely at the expense of others will probably have to pay the cost himself in the long run; for those who hear him will fear him, and will retire into themselves in his presence. On the other hand, nothing is more honourable than to stand forth as the defender or the palliator of the faults imputed to others, and nothing is easier than to expand such a defence into general considerations as to the purity of human motives, which will raise the conversation from its unwholesome ground into the upper air.

If the company be fit for it, no general rule is more valuable than that of turning the conversation away from people and fixing it on things; but, alas! How many there are who only take interest in people, and in the weakest and most trivial aspects of people! Few things are more essential and more neglected in the education of children than to habituate them to talk about things, and not people; yet, what use is there in urging these more special rules, when the very idea of teaching them to converse at all is foreign to the minds of most parents and of all educators?

It will be conceded that the one thing absolutely essential to the education of a lady is that she should talk agreeably at meals. It is the natural meeting time, not only of the house hold, but of friends, and conversation is then as essential as food. Yet, what is the habit of many of our schools? They either enforce silence at this period, or they compel the wretched pupils to speak in a foreign language, in which they can only labour out spasmodic commonplaces, without any interchange or play of thought. Consequently, many of us drift into the habit of regarding meal times as the precise occasion when conversation is impossible. How far this malediction, during some of the most critical years of their lives, affects them permanently, it is not easy to overestimate.

If You Can Talk Well

There is no other thing which enables us to make so good an impression, especially upon those who do not know us thoroughly, as the ability to converse well.

To be a good conversationalist, able to interest people, rivet their attention, draw them to you naturally, by the very superiority of your conversational ability, is to be the possessor of a very great accomplishment, one which is superior to all others. It not only helps you to make a good impression upon strangers, it also helps you to make and keep friends. It opens doors and softens hearts. It makes you interesting in all sorts of company. It helps you to get on in the world. It sends you clients, patients, customers. It helps you into the best society, even though you are poor.

A man who can talk well, who has the art of putting things in an attractive way, who can interest others immediately by his power of speech, has a very great advantage over one who may know more than he, but who cannot express himself with ease or eloquence.

You may be a fine singer, and yet travel around the world without having an opportunity of showing your accomplishment, or without guessing your specialty. But wherever you go, and in whatever society you are, no matter what your station in life may be, you talk.

You may be a painter, you may have spent years with great masters, and yet, unless you have very marked ability so that your pictures are hung in the salons or in the great art galleries, comparatively few people will ever see them. But if you are an artist in conversation, everyone who comes in contact with you will see your life picture, which you have been painting ever since you began to talk. Everyone knows whether you are an artist or a bungler.

Nothing else will indicate your fineness or coarseness of culture, your breeding or lack of it, so quickly as your conversation. It will tell your whole life's story. What you say, and how you say it, will betray all your secrets, will give the world your true measure.

There is no other accomplishment or acquirement which you can use so constantly and effectively, which will give so much pleasure to your friends, as fine conversation. There is no doubt that the gift of language was intended to be a much greater accomplishment than the majority of us have ever made of it.

Most of us are bunglers in our conversation, because we do not make an art of it; we do not take the trouble or pains to learn to talk well. We do not read enough or think enough. Most of us express ourselves in sloppy, slipshod English, because it is so much easier to do so than it is to think before we speak, to make an effort to express ourselves with elegance, ease, and power.

Poor conversers excuse themselves for not trying to improve by saying that good talkers are born, not made. We might as well say that good lawyers, good physicians, or good merchants are born, not made. None of them would ever get very far without hard work. This is the price of all achievement that is of value.

Few people think very much about how they are going to express themselves. They use the first words that come to them. They do not think of forming a sentence so that it will have beauty, brevity, transparency, power. The words flow from their lips helter-skelter, with little thought of arrangement or order.

Now and then we meet a real artist in conversation, and it is such a treat and delight that we wonder why most of us should be such bunglers in our conversation, that we should make such a botch of the medium of communication between human beings, when it is capable of being made the art of arts.

In olden times the art of conversation reached a much higher standard than that of today. The deterioration is due to the complete revolution in the conditions of modern civilisation. Formerly people had almost no other way of communicating their thoughts than by speech. Knowledge of all kinds was disseminated almost wholly through the spoken word. There were no great daily newspapers, no magazines or periodicals of any kind.

The great discoveries of vast wealth in the precious minerals, the new world opened up by inventions and discoveries, and the great impetus to ambition have changed all this. In this lightning-express age, in these strenuous times, when everybody has a mania to attain wealth and position, we no longer have time to reflect with deliberation, and to develop our powers of conversation. In these great newspaper and periodical days, when everybody can get for one or a few cents the news and information which it has cost thousands of dollars to collect, everybody sits behind the morning sheet or is buried in a book or magazine. There is no longer the same need of communicating thought by the spoken word, as there was formerly.

Oratory is becoming a lost art for the same reason. Printing has become so cheap that even the poorest homes can get more reading for a few dollars than kings and noblemen could afford in the Middle Ages.

It is a rare thing to find a polished conversationalist today. So rare is it to hear one speaking exquisite English, and using a superb diction, that it is indeed a luxury.

Good reading, however, will not only broaden the mind and give new ideas, but it will also increase one's vocabulary, and that is a great aid to conversation. Many people have good thoughts and ideas, but they cannot express them because of the poverty of their vocabulary. They have not words enough to clothe their ideas and make them attractive. They talk around in a circle, repeat and repeat, because, when they want a particular word to convey their exact meaning, they cannot find it.

Many people, especially scholars, seem to think that the great desideratum in life is to get as much valuable information into the head as possible. But it is just as important to know how to give out knowledge in a palatable manner as to acquire it. You may be a profound scholar, you may be well read in history and in politics, you may be wonderfully well posted in science, literature, and art, and yet, if your knowledge is locked up within you, you will always be placed at a great disadvantage.

Locked-up ability may give the individual some satisfaction, but it must be exhibited, expressed in some attractive, way, before the world will appreciate it or give credit for it. It does not matter how valuable the rough diamond may be, no explaining, no describing its marvels of beauty within, and its great value, would avail; nobody would appreciate it until it was ground and polished and the light let into its depths to reveal its hidden brilliancy. Conversation is to the man what the cutting of the diamond is to the stone. The grinding does not add anything to the diamond.

It merely reveals its wealth. How little parents realise the harm they are doing their children by allowing them to grow up ignorant of or indifferent to the marvelous possibilities in the art of conversation! In the majority of homes, children are allowed to mangle the English language in a most painful way.

Nothing else will develop the brain and character more than the constant effort to talk well, intelligently, interestingly, upon all sorts of topics. There is a splendid discipline in the constant effort to express one's thoughts in clear language and in an interesting manner. We know people who are such superb conversers that no one would ever dream that they have not had the advantages of the higher schools. Many a college graduate has been silenced and put to shame by people who have never even been to a high school, but who have studied the art of self-expression.

The school and the college employ the student comparatively a few hours a day for a few years; conversation is a training in a perpetual school. Many get the best part of their education in this school.

Conversation is a great ability discoverer, a great revealer of possibilities and resources. It stimulates thought wonderfully. We think more of ourselves if we can talk well, if we can interest and hold others. The power to do so increases our self-respect and our self-confidence.

No man knows what he really possesses until he makes his best effort to express to others what is in him. Then the avenues of the mind fly open, the faculties are on the alert. Every good converser has felt a power come to him from the listener which he never felt before, and which often stimulates and inspires to fresh endeavor. The mingling of thought with thought, the contact of mind with mind, develops new powers, as the mixing of two chemicals produces a new third substance.

To converse well one must listen well also. This means one must hold oneself in a receptive attitude.

One cause for our conversational decline is a lack of sympathy. We are too selfish, too busily engaged in our own welfare, and wrapped up in our own little world, too intent upon our own self-promotion to be interested in others. No one can make a good converser who is not sympathetic. You must be able to enter into another's life, to live it with the other person, in order to be a good talker or a good listener, Lincoln was master of the art of making himself interesting to everybody he met. He put people at ease with his stories and jokes, and made them feel so completely at home in his presence that they opened up their mental treasures to him without reserve. Strangers were always glad to talk with him, because he was so cordial and quaint, and always gave more than he got.

A sense of humour such as Lincoln had is, of course, a great addition to one's conversational powers. But not everyone can be funny; and, if you lack the sense of humour, you will make yourself ludicrous by attempting to be so.

A good conversationalist, however, is not too serious. He does not deal too much with facts, no matter how important. Vivacity is absolutely necessary. Heavy, conversation bores; too light, disgusts.

Therefore, to be a good conversationalist you must be spontaneous, buoyant, natural, sympathetic, and must show a spirit of good will. You must feel a spirit of helpfulness, and must enter heart and soul into things which interest others. You must get the attention of people and hold it by interesting them, and you can only interest them by a warm sympathy -a real friendly sympathy. If you are cold, distant, and unsympathetic, you cannot hold their attention.

You must bring your listener close to you, must open your

heart wide, and exhibit a broad, free nature, and an open mind. You must be responsive, so that he will throw wide open every avenue of his nature and give you free access to his heart of hearts.

If a man is a success anywhere, it ought to be in his personality, in his power to express himself in strong, effective, interesting language. He should not be obliged to give a stranger an inventory of his possessions in order to show that he has achieved something. A greater wealth should flow from his lips, and express itself in his manner.

No amount of natural ability, or education or good clothes, no amount of money, will make you appear well if you cannot express yourself in good language.

CHAPTER 11

A Culture of Conversation

Nothing clarifies our ideas on any subject like subjecting them to the white heat of free discussion; nothing gives us so clear a knowledge of our own powers as measuring them with those of others. And sometimes we find that in endeavouring to receive light we do so by the action of our own minds, and shed more light than we receive. Many a man has acquired clearer intellectual light on his own talents, gained more confidence in himself, by mixing among men and comparing himself with others, than in any other way.

True conversation is always reciprocally beneficial. No matter how much you give, you are sure to receive something; no matter how much you receive, you are sure to give something. The more you give, the more you have to give. Expression of thought makes it grow. As soon as you express one thought, a hundred others may start from it; the avenues of the mind open at once to new views, to new perceptions of things; fresh beams of light flash in on all sides, each beam enabling you to see things you never saw before; so that, by a compensating law in the intellectual as in the moral life, the giver is more blessed than the receiver. And, far from impoverishing him, the more he distributes his wealth, the wealthier he becomes; for he may say with Juliet:

"The more I give to thee, The more I have."

A new thought to the thinker may be simply a new thought

and nothing more–a dear germ waiting for the contact of another thought to be warmed into life. By dropping it into the mind of another, it suddenly germinates and springs into life; it expands and grows into a new creation.

Thought produces thought, and he who sits down to write a letter sometimes finds himself expanding into an essay or a history. Burke's famous Reflections on the French Revolution originated in a letter to a young friend.

He had no sooner begun to state his views to his friend than the subject began to expand on all sides, showing its far-reaching influences and effects. His young friend had touched a spring that unlocked a whole mine of golden ore.

Coleridge's most famous poem, the 'Ancient Mariner,' was suggested by a remark of Wordsworth's in conversation. The two men had been talking of writing a poem in which a supernatural event might be related in such a way as to give it a resemblance of truth; whereupon Coleridge related the dream of a friend in which a skeleton ship was navigated by dead men; then Wordsworth said he had been reading of a ship in the South Seas which, after one of the crew had shot an albatross, was tossed about in storms or spellbound in calms, the killing of the seabird being supposed to arouse the ire of the tutelary spirits of that region.

Thus, the 'Ancient Mariner' arose from the single remark of a friend in conversation. "The gloss with which it was subsequently accompanied," says Wordsworth, "was not thought of by either of us at the time; at least not a hint of it was given to me; so I have no doubt it was a felicitous afterthought."

Of course, the suggestion was all that the poet needed to build upon; for when his fertile mind had got to work, the rest followed easily.

And curiously enough, it was in a similar way that an American poet received the first suggestion for his greatest and most popular work. "Hawthorne dined one day with Longfellow," says Mr. James T. Fields, "and brought a friend with him from Salem. After dinner, the friend said, "I have been trying to persuade Hawthorne to write a story based on a legend of Arcadia, and still current there–the legend of a girl who, in the dispersion of the Arcadians, was separated from her lover, passed her life in waiting and seeking for him, and only found him at last dying in a hospital when both were old."

Longfellow wondered that the legend did not strike the fancy of Hawthorne, and he said to him, "If you have really made up your mind not to use it for a story, will you let me have it for a poem?" To this, Hawthorne readily consented, and promised moreover not to treat the subject in prose till Longfellow had seen what he could do with it in verse."

No talent is more admirable than that of the man who knows how to touch those hidden springs which set quiet and undemonstrative people a-talking-those taciturn people who never speak except when they are spoken to or have something worth telling. There are always subjects about which such people can talk most interestingly if they can only be induced to speak.

He who has the power of drawing people out, who has that confiding, amiable, and pleasing manner which dispels reserve and self-consciousness, which puts people at ease and inspires them with speech and a willingness to talk, has a master talent, which is as rare as it is valuable.

In whatever company such a man appears, his presence acts like sunshine on plants; every one finds himself expanding with new life, and ready to exhibit whatever element of beauty or refinement there is in him. Touching their minds in that light, airy, quickening way which stirs thought and recollection, he dispels reserve and inspires confidence; and thus he causes the company to vie with each other in telling things that are amusing or instructive, or that elucidate whatever subject is discussed.

To quote Waters "Most men, even those well informed, think little of what they have learned, and much of what they still have to learn; the field of knowledge constantly widens before them, while that which they have gone through seems comparatively limited; but it is by showing what they know that they learn more, and gain distinctness and clearness in the knowledge they have. And sometimes a plain man condenses a whole life experience in a few spoken sentences."

CHAPTER 12

Improving Conversation in Special Situations

There are many 'unwritten' rules that we take for granted. These rules if taught to children right at the start, lead to a cultured development of their ability to conversate.

Taking Turns

Children with delayed language or social skills may not take their turn properly in conversations. They often don't respond to indirect questions or instructions, such as I wish someone would tell me what time it is. They may have poor language comprehension skills, too, making it difficult for them to respond consistently.

Starting a Conversation

It is important to model appropriate ways for your child to approach other children. If you see that your child is interested in joining another child or children, suggest a way to start the conversation: e.g., "Hi. Can I play with you?" It sounds very simple, but for a child who has difficulty using words, you make it much easier by modelling the correct words, grammar, and pronunciation for them.

Staying On Topic Or Changing To A New Topic Appropriately

It is common for children with weak language skills to have

difficulty staying on topic in conversation, and it is also hard for them to explain connections between topics. For example, in a conversation about the zoo, a child may say My car is blue. This may be off-topic, or there may be a connection that isn't apparent (Maybe it was hard to find the car in the parking lot at the zoo). Just re-state the topic (We're talking about the zoo now, was your car at the zoo?), and keep repeating the topic as needed.

Making Eye Contact

For a child with poor attention control or weak comprehension skills, it is very important that they look at the person they are talking to. For children who seem 'tuned out' or in a world of their own, making eye contact is the first step in connecting with other people.

Understanding Personal Space

People are very uncomfortable when others stand too close or too far away. Use reminders, and play silly games where you and your child try to talk from too close and too far, so you can talk about how hard it is to listen that way.

Reading Other People's Body Language

The same way a child with language difficulties has trouble understanding oral language, they may have trouble responding to 'social' or nonverbal language. Again, make a game with exaggerated expressions and gestures, asking your child to guess what message you are sending.

Children usually use their first words between 9 and 18 months of age. Some children are late in starting to talk, or they stay at a 'first words' stage for a long time.

If you are concerned about your child's speech development, ask your doctor for a referral to a speech-language pathologist. In the meantime, here are key strategies for helping your child to use more words.

Listen

Before children use words to communicate, they often use gestures, grunts, or part-words. Don't ignore these. Interpret them as words, modelling the word your child would say if they could. So, if your child reaches for the milk and says uhh, answer back, Milk? Oh, you want milk. By listening, you follow their lead; your words are much more meaningful to them when you talk about a topic they picked.

Wait, then wait some more

It takes children a long time to formulate words and sounds. Try not to anticipate your children's needs. Even if they just use a grunt to tell you they need something, you've given them a chance to take their turn in the conversation. Silence is okay – give children enough time to respond to you or to initiate a conversation.

Repeat, repeat, repeat

Children need to hear a word in many different sentences and in many different situations to learn all about that word. Play repetitive games with simple words, such as open and shut, or up and down. Children will first use a new word in a familiar routine because using that word will be predictable and automatic in that routine.

Expand and add language

When children do use a word, repeat it back to them, adding a simple word or sentence to it. So, if your child says ball!, respond Yes – it's a big ball. or, You're right! Ball. Let's play with the ball. This lets them know that you are listening to them and adds information to the topic that is holding their interest.

Model good speech

Talk clearly and slowly with a lot of animation in your voice. Your child will be able to understand you more easily and will also mimic your clear speech. You can still speak to them in 'adult' sentences, just pause at natural breaks in the sentence. Pausing before saying a word gets the listeners' attention and adds emphasis to the word (e.g., I think we should go to the... playground!)

Speech and Language Disorders

Improving Vocabulary Skills

Playing games involving word-association and categorisation helps children to organise vocabulary they already know (but may have trouble recalling at times), and to build a framework in which to learn new words.

- Opposites (hot/cold, big/little, dirty/clean, over/under, etc.)

  For example: sort objects into 'wet' and 'not wet' categories, talking about all those that are 'not wet' being 'dry'

- Adjectives (round, rough, orange, funny, etc.)

  For example: find all the objects in the room that are 'soft'

- Functions (household items, farm machinery, etc.)

  For example: guess the name of hidden pictures by listening to what they do ('something that cleans the floor')

- Categories ('food', 'clothes', 'toys', etc.)

  For example: play 'shopping' by sorting pictures into the stores they belong in - pet store/grocery store

- 'What doesn't belong?'

  For example: apple, cracker, banana, and elephant - which one is not like the others?

- Describe hidden objects

  For example: play 'I spy' in the car, listing all the characteristics of objects for others to guess

- Parts of objects (door, lock, hinge, knocker, etc.)

For example: draw parts of an object on a piece of paper, one by one, until the other person guesses what it is

- Places (hospital, restaurant, zoo, etc.)

For example: pack a school bag, discussing what you do and do not need at school

The Difficult to Understand Child

Talking with a child who is difficult to understand can be frustrating for both of you. Here are some suggestions for making your conversations more relaxed and successful:

- Keep your own speech slow and clearly enunciated.
- Repeat back the parts of their message that you understood.
- When you understand what the child said, repeat it back to them.
- Try not to pretend to understand if you really don't understand.

Keep your own speech slow and clearly enunciated

The same way children will whisper automatically if you speak to them in a whisper, they will copy your speaking style. Don't tell them to slow down or to speak more clearly – they can't control their speech as easily as adults can – this often just frustrates them further or makes them want to stop talking altogether.

Repeat back the parts of their message that you understood

You're telling me something about a dog – what did the dog do?

This lets them know that you are listening to them and are trying to understand. It also means that when they fill in the part that you didn't understand they will probably be using a single word or a short phrase – the shorter the sentence, the easier they will be to understand.

When you understand what the child said, repeat it back to them:

Child: Look - a tar go bas

Adult: Wow - the car does go fast!

This shows your child the correct way to pronounce the words they used, while letting them know that you understood what they said. Don't make them repeat the correct pronunciation back to you too often – it will make them less likely to try difficult words in the future if they're worried about being constantly corrected.

Try not to pretend to understand if you really don't understand

Children often know if you're bluffing and can just get more frustrated. Nodding and saying 'yes' to everything they say makes it difficult for them to figure out what is right and wrong, too.

Find the patterns in their errors

Try to find patterns in your child's speech - Do they always substitute a 'w' sound for a 'l' sound? Do they use 'baby talk' when they get tired or sick? If you understand the patterns in their speech, it will be easier to guess what they are saying, and you can help them try to break the patterns.

Practice

Practice individual words and sentences during a special 'speech time' (with materials provided by your speech-language pathologist).

Rhyms

Practice lots of rhymes, rhyming stories, and songs, clapping with the rhythm (you can't skip syllables in rhymes).

Grammatical Errors

When children aren't using correct grammar, their speech is much more difficult to follow, even if they are making most of the sounds correctly.

Them's can cut for it? for Can they cut with it?

To Help

Use good grammar and repeat their words back to them with the correct grammar.

CHAPTER 13

Daily Conversation

Here are a few examples of daily conversation that will give you a glimpse of how conversation takes place.

You can count on me

Kiran	Simran, can you drive Jane and me to the doctor on Monday?
Simran	I think so.
Kiran	We need a ride very badly, are you sure you will be able to help out?
Simran	Sure. I will mark it on my calendar so I don't forget.
Kiran	Thanks you are a good friend.
Simran	**You can** always **count on me** when you need help.

It is up to you

Jatin	Would you like to go out to dinner or to a movie?
Karan	Either one, **it is up to you.**
Jatin	What would you prefer?
Karan	I really don't care; I just want to get out of the house.
Jatin	Well, then how about dinner and a movie?
Karan	That's a great idea!

I couldn't help it

Varun	I am upset. Somebody told my boss I have a part-time job.
Dhruv	And he doesn't like that?
Varun	No, he doesn't. He thinks that I am too tired to work.
Dhruv	I am sorry. I have to admit I told him.
Varun	You told him? Why?
Dhruv	**I couldn't help it**. He asked me point-blank.

It's better than nothing

Mahesh	Did you ask Mr. Davidson for a raise?
Manu	Yes, I asked for an appraisal of Rs. 3,000.
Mahesh	Did you get it?
Manu	No, I got only 1000.
Mahesh	That's too bad.
Manu	Oh, it is alright. **It is better than nothing**.

It doesn't make any difference

Mohit	Shall I pick you up at 5 or 6?
Joei	**It doesn't make any difference**.
Mohit	O.K I will pick you up at 5.
Joei	No problem!
Mohit	Shall we play badminton or table tennis this weekend?
Joei	**It doesn't make any difference**.

Chances are slim

Carol	What are your chances of getting through the entrance exam?
Kiran	My **chances are slim**.

Carol	I hear those colleges are tough to get into.
Kiran	I know. I'd have better chance at Meerut University.
Carol	Sure. It's not a bad either.
Kiran	I'd rather be a big fish in a small pond.

It is on the tip of my tongue

Vaibhav	Do you remember the restaurant we went to Friday?
Ishan	Sure I do. It was the Silver Castle.
Vaibhav	No, we've never been to the Silver Castle.
Ishan	Maybe it was the Gold Coin.
Vaibhav	No Gee. **It is on the tip of my tongue.**
Ishan	Never mind. The food was terrible.

Not that I know of

Mei	Is Mrs. Johnson joining us for dinner?
Susie	**Not that I know of.**
Mei	I was hoping she would come with us.
Susie	Why?
Mei	I would like her to try some of the traditional Chinese foods.
Susie	That's very kind of you

It's a piece of cake

Prayag	What kind of Chinese food would you like to have?
Nitish	I'd like to have spring rolls.
Prayag	Fine. By the way, do you know how to use chopsticks?
Nitish	**It's a piece of cake.**
Prayag	How in the world did you learn to use them?
Nitish	I was stationed in Taiwan for five years, you know.

I tossed and turned all night

Jack	Are you ill?
Siddharth	Not really! I am just tired.
Jack	Didn't you sleep well last night.
Siddharth	No, **I tossed and turned all night**.
Jack	I am sorry to hear that, I hope you sleep better tonight.
Siddharth	Thank you. I'm sure I will.

Let's get to the point

Divya	Good afternoon Arun, isn't it a lovely day?
Arun	Yes, it is Divya!
Divya	It is the kind of day when you want to go outside.
Arun	Divya, **let's get to the point**. Do you want the afternoon off?
Divya	Yes, Arun.
Arun	Alright. As soon as you finish typing. You can go.

Does it ring a bell

Shirley	Guess who I met at the grocery store!
Sidd	I can't imagine.
Shirley	Do you remember Mr. Johnson from our old neighbourhood.
Sidd	That name **rings a bell**, but **I can't place him**.
Shirley	He used to live in the building next to ours.
Sidd	Oh yes, now I remember. He had dark hair and wore glasses.

I'll keep my fingers crossed

Peters	Please have a seat.
Albert	Thank you!

Peters	I'm Mr. Peters. The personnel manager. What can I do for you?
Albert	I am looking for a position as a sales representative.
Peters	We may have an opening next week. Please leave your resume, I will keep in touch with you.
Albert	Thanks. **I'll keep my fingers crossed.**

Don't get me wrong

Kunal	Bill is going to sing tonight.
Geeta	Oh, no!
Kunal	Don't you like his singing?
Geeta	It's not that. **Don't get me wrong**
Kunal	What's the problem then?
Geeta	He only knows one song.

Out of the question

Karan	I am going to look at new cars tomorrow.
Peter	I wish I could have one.
Karan	Why don't you come along?
Peter	I'd like to but I don't want to be tempted.
Karan	I am sure you could get a good deal.
Peter	No, buying a new car is **out of the question** for me right now.

I am broke

James	Are you going to Hawaii on your vacation?
Phagun	Not this year.
James	Why not?
Phagun	For a good reason, **I am broke.**

| James | Oh! Come on. |
| Phagun | Seriously, I am flat broke. |

Brush up on

Jeff	Do you have a driver's license?
Mike	No. I am going to take the test in a couple of weeks.
Jeff	Didn't you drive in your country?
Mike	Yes, but I have to **brush up on** my driving.
Jeff	And. You have to study the traffic rules too!
Mike	Yes, there is a lot of new things I must learn.

Rain Check

Ritika	My brother and his family will be coming into town next week.
Nitish	Is he the one who writes articles for the English Post?
Ritika	Right, why don't you come over next Sunday to meet him?
Nitish	I'd love to but I can't. Can you give me a **rain check?**
Ritika	Sure, they'll be here for a week. So just let me know when you can come.
Nitish	Ok! I will be very interested in seeing him.

I am starving

Paras	I think we should get something to eat.
Vaibhavi	Are you hungry?
Paras	Hungry? **I'm starving**.
Vaibhavi	There is an Italian restaurant near here.
Paras	Is the food very hot?
Vaibhavi	It's kind of hot, but it's very tasty.

Whatever you say

Kat	How about having dinner together after work?
Mori	Fine.
Kat	Should we have Japanese or American food?
Mori	**Whatever you say!**
Kat	There is a good steak house around the corner.
Mori	That's a good idea.

It's beyond me

Keshav	How long have you been in this country?
Sarthak	Two months.
Keshav	Is he hard for you to study at an American college?
Sarthak	Yes, I find it very difficult. Especially when you can't follow the professor's lecture.
Keshav	That's because you just arrived. Do you like biology?
Sarthak	No. **It's beyond me.**

You are on the right track

Rishabh	I am trying to figure out who the murderer is in this story.
Harsh	Who do you think it is!
Rishabh	I think it's Mr. Johnson because he was in the house at the time of the murder.
Harsh	No, but you **are on the right track**.

You can say that again

Paras	I think there is a sharp contrast between Americans and Chinese. For example the Americans are very individualistic, while the Chinese are very group-oriented.

Sam   You can say that again. Chinese are very conscious of what other people think of them.

Don't get me wrong

Marcie   **Don't get me wrong!** I think Calvin is a very nice person, but you have to admit he isn't very responsible.

Prakash   I think you are right, he has got a lot of growing up to do.

Give it to me straight

Boss   As you know Mukesh, you are a highly-valued worker. However, the company has run into financial difficulty lately that are causing some unexpected repercussions.

Mukesh   Like what! **Give it to me straight**.

Boss   I am afraid we have to lay you off.

I'll tell you what

Dave   Let's go to the movies in Prickly tomorrow.

Kun   Ok, where should we meet. Do you know where Lot 10 is? We went there together.

Dave   No, I don't remember. Let's meet somewhere outside Prickly.

Kun   **I'll tell you what** — name the place and I'll pick you up.

In a row

Jane   The new year will be here before you know it.

Mei   This year really went by fast.

Jane   It seems every year goes by faster.

Mei   I especially enjoy the new year, though.

Jane	Why?
Mei	We have three holidays **in a row**.

In the air

Jenny	Deepti! Guess what. Leo proposed to me!
Deepti	Wow. Love is **in the air**. Did you accept?
Jenny	Not yet. I have some doubts...like the age factor. I'm really robbing the cradle here.
Deepti	So he's eight years younger...he's mature for his age.
Jenny	I'm worried about the cultural differences, too.
Deepti	You guys have the same interests and similar personalities. And you have the same dreams.

Don't flatter yourself

Ritika	What is that noise?
Vardhan	What noise?
Ritika	I hear a girl saying "Vardhan, honey. Please pick up the phone, you stud..."
Vardhan	Oh! That's my new cell phone. It must be my latest squeeze, Jane.
Ritika	Jane?
Vardhan	Yeah. She's totally into me. She calls me all the time.
Ritika	**Don't flatter yourself!**

He is a good catch

Nitish	Guess who else is falling into the love trap!
Smriti	It better not be Bobbie. I don't want to lose another friend to the death of love.
Nitish	It's Marie. With the guy from New York..
Smriti	No wonder! I saw her wearing a promise ring.
Nitish	I encouraged her. I think **he's a good catch**.

| Smriti | It better not be just because he looks like Tom Cruise. Marriage is more than a fling with a movie-star look-alike. |

Work like a charm

Salesman	Lowest prices! Best quality! Hello, sir!
Buyer	Oh, hi. I'm just looking. I have a computer already.
Salesman	How long have you had it?
Buyer	Years. **Works like a charm.**
Salesman	Years? What a dinosaur! I can't believe you still use it.
Buyer	It's fine for writing letters and...

My battery must be low

Aarti	Hello?
Lokesh	Hi it's me what's up baby? I'm sorry! Listen! I'm going to be late tonight so don't stay up and wait for me OK?
Aarti	Where are you?
Lokesh	Wait wait! Say that again?
Aarti	Hello?
Lokesh	You're coming in and out I think my **battery must be low.** Listen! If you can hear me we're going to a place nearby, alright? Got to go. (*click*)

She just seems to have the knack

Minal	I'm so envious of Radhika's cooking.
Anne	Me too, everything she does tastes perfect.
Minal	I tried some of her recipes myself, but they just don't seem to turn out right.
Anne	You're not the only one, I tried to make her Black

Forest cake the other day. It tasted all right but not half as good as Radhika's.

Minal	How does she do it I wonder?
Anne	**She just seems to have the knack.**

Go at steady pace

Peter	Where are you going on the weekend?
Vardhan	I'm going hiking with some classmate.
Peter	Hiking? Isn't that rather strenuous?
Vardhan	Not if you **go at a steady pace** and take the occasional break.
Peter	Oh, that doesn't sound too bad.
Vardhan	Why don't you join us? You'll have a great time.

Let's go for a spin

Pankaj	I'm feeling energetic today. **Let's go for a spin.**
Arun	OK. I need some exercise.
Pankaj	Where shall we go?
Arun	Let's go around the lake, over the hill and come back through the wood.
Pankaj	Fine, that's about 15 kilometers, enough for one day.
Arun	Don't forget your puncture outfit and crash helmet.

Stick at it

Rahul	Don't you find these rowing machines hard work?
Vardhan	I certainly do, but they're supposed to be.
Rahul	How often do you come to the gym for a workout?
Vardhan	Three times a week at least if I can manage it.
Rahul	No wonder you look so fit and trim.
Vardhan	Thanks. **Stick at it** and you can be the same.

It really gets up my nose

Prakash	It's been a pretty tight game so far, don't you think?
Sanju	Yes, neither side have looked like scoring a goal so far.
Prakash	Except that one time when our striker was almost through but was fouled by the fullback. The referee didn't see it.
Sanju	Yes, **it really gets up my nose** when something like that happens.
Prakash	Well, let's hope that the ref will be looking right way if that fullback tries playing dirty again.
Sanju	And then we'll get a penalty.

They've probably been held up by the traffic

Tom	You're not looking too cheerful.
Henry	Well, I arranged with Aron and Rahul to meet me here for a drink at seven o'clock. It's now a quarter to eight and neither of them has turned up.
Tom	I wouldn't give up hope. **They've probably been held up by the traffic.** It's been very heavy for the past hour.
Henry	Even so, they should have turned up by now.
Tom	Well, I'd give them another quarter of an hour or so.
Henry	OK, but after that I'm going home.

My luggage went astray

Gul	I had a terrible time on my last trip to Europe.
Sachin	Why, what happened? Did you have an accident?
Gul	No, **my luggage went astray**. When I arrived in Paris and went to collect my case from the baggage carousel, it never arrived.

Sachin	What happened to it? Had somebody collected it by mistake or stolen it?
Gul	No, it had been sent on to Karnataka by mistake.
Sachin	Did you get it back?
Gul	Yes I did, but it took two whole days. I was absolutely furious.

He kept changing channels on the remote

Sharon	My mother got really annoyed with my father yesterday evening.
Kanu	Why, did he complain about her cooking?
Sharon	Oh no, she's a great cook. It was when they were watching television.
Kanu	Don't tell me he fell asleep in front of the television and started snoring.
Sharon	No, he does that sometimes but this was because **he kept changing channels on the remote.**
Kanu	All men do that, it's one of their most annoying habits.

He's clearly over the moon about something

Dheeraj	Have you seen Johnny today?
Sanju	No, why?
Dheeraj	Well **he's clearly over the moon about something.**
Sanju	What about?
Dheeraj	He won't tell anybody, but I've never seen him looking so happy.
Sanju	He's a betting man, so perhaps he's won a lot of money on the horses.

They seem to have a lot in common

Esha	Mandy and Sumit seem to be spending a lot of time together lately.
Neel	Yes that's true. I've seen them at the swimming pool lately and at the cinema.
Esha	They go on regular bike rides together too.
Neel	**They seem to have a lot in common.**
Esha	Yes, they clearly like the same things.
Neel	I wonder if we'll be hearing wedding bells soon.

Started a new hobby

Rachna	My sister **started a new hobby** a few months ago.
Heather	Really? Tell me more.
Rachna	She's been learning to paint watercolors.
Heather	How interesting. What are her favorite subjects?
Rachna	She likes painting landscapes best, but she also enjoys doing still lifes.
Heather	I envy her. I've tried to paint in the past, but I'm no good - I have no artistic talent.

She sight-reads really well

Clare	My elder sister is always in demand at family parties.
Angie	Why, is she a good singer?
Clare	No, she plays the piano really well and she can play whatever music anyone puts in front of her.
Angie	I can play the piano, but I couldn't do that. How does she do it?
Clare	**She sight-reads really well.**
Angie	I wish I could do that, it's a great skill.

The Real goalie made a fantastic save

Sameer	Did you see the Barcelona-Real Madrid match on TV yesterday?
Vivek	Of course, what a game! Three goals each.
Sameer	Who do you support?
Vivek	Real Madrid, because I'm a Beckham fan.
Sameer	Barcelona should have won it with that great shot on goal in the last minute.
Vivek	Only they didn't because **the real goalie made a fantastic save.**

I like the way you pan across the ruins

Harbans	Your vacation video is really interesting.
Sachin	Well, Mexico is a fascinating country.
Harbans	What are we looking at now?
Sachin	These are the remains of a Mayan city.
Harbans	**I like the way you pan across the ruins** very slowly.
Sachin	That helps you to see what a really large area they cover.

I wish I could play the piano like you

Andy	**I wish I could play the piano like you.**
Dee	I'm sure you could if you tried. You should take some lessons.
Andy	I took some when I was younger but I was hopeless.
Dee	Why was that?
Andy	I found that I was tone-deaf, which really made it impossible.
Dee	Never mind, why don't you try learning the drums? Then being tone-deaf shouldn't matter.

She's got a really green thumb

Akhilesh	What a beautiful garden your parents have!
Ronak	I'm glad you like it. They certainly spend a lot of time on it.
Akhilesh	And the houseplants are also very attractive.
Ronak	They're my mother's specialty. Some of them are nearly twenty years old.
Akhilesh	Good heavens, how does she do it?
Ronak	**She's got a really green thumb**; plants seem to respond to her.

My sister's hobby is dress making

Swati	You look slimmer than when I saw you last.
Kajal	Yes, I must have lost six pounds over the last two months. My best dress is now too big for me. I can't wear it any more.
Swati	Don't say that, I think I can help you.
Kajal	How do you mean?
Swati	Well, **my sister's hobby is dress making** and I'm sure she wouldn't mind taking it in so that it'll fit you again. I'll ask her.
Kajal	That would be fantastic. I'm no good at sewing myself.

She's got a really useful right foot

John	My sister's really keen on soccer.
Eric	Really, what team does she support.
John	She doesn't support any in particular. When I say keen, I mean she's an enthusiastic player. She plays for a local women's team.
Eric	Is she any good?

| John | Well, she's scored ten goals so far this season. **She's got a really useful right foot.** |
| Eric | Well if that's the case, you really must take me to see her play sometime. |

What a bargain

Jenny	Look what I've got.
Sid	Wow, that's the snazziest looking handbag I've ever seen. Where did you get it?
Jenny	I got it in Paris on my last trip.
Sid	I bet it cost a fortune?
Jenny	No it didn't, I got it for half price because the shop was having a clearance sale.
Sid	**What a bargain!** You'll have to take me with you next time.

You've been ripped off

Tarun	What do you think of my new suit?
Vishal	Not bad. I like the wide lapels and the pant cuffs. It reminds me of one I saw in the department store the other day. Did you get it there?
Tarun	No, I got it at that new outfitters on the main street.
Vishal	How much did it cost?
Tarun	Three hundred and fifty dollars.
Vishal	What? You could have got the one from the department store for Rs. 2,000. **You've been ripped off!**

My feet are killing me

| Marie | You look a bit tired. What have you been doing? |
| Neel | Shopping for some new outfits. |

Marie	Did you get what you want?
Neel	I did, but it took me all day.
Marie	What do you want to do now?
Neel	I just want to sit down somewhere and relax. **My feet are killing me!**

I've got it on thirty days' free trial

Neena	Why are you talking to your computer? Is it lonely?
David	No, don't be silly, I'm trying out some new speech recognition software.
Neena	How does it work?
David	Well, I just speak what I want to say into the microphone and my words appear on the screen. It's magic!
Neena	It must be very expensive.
David	It's not cheap but I haven't actually paid anything yet.
Neena	How come?
David	**I've got it on thirty days' free trial.** If I'm not satisfied with it, I can return it free of charge as long as I do so within 30 days.

She is impossible to please

First clerk	I've just had a terrible hour and a half.
Second clerk	Why, what happened?
First clerk	Well I had a lady customer come in who wanted to buy a pair of shoes. And you know we've got a really good range.
Second clerk	We certainly do. Did she buy a pair?
First clerk	No, but she didn't leave before getting me to bring her every single pair we had in the

shop. And she complained about every single one.

Second clerk   I'd say **she was impossible to please.**

He's a thoroughbred boxer with an outstanding pedigree

Parag   Is that your new dog?

Shailendra Yes, we've only had him a week.

Parag   He's really handsome and very lively.

Shailendra He should be, he cost a fortune.

Parag   Why was he so expensive?

Shailendra **He's a thoroughbred Boxer with an outstanding pedigree** that's why. We got him from a top breeder.

Parag   Do you intend to show him?

Shailendra We're not sure; we'll take a breeder's advice on that.

Our cat had a litter

Neelam   What a playful litter kitten! Is it a boy or a girl?

Divya   It's a girl. We've decided to call her Winkie.

Neelam   How sweet! How old is she?

Divya   Only six weeks.

Neelam   Did you get her from a pet shop?

Divya   No, **our cat had a litter** for four and she's the only one left.

Neelam   What do you mean?

Divya   Well we've given the other three to friends but decided to keep her, as she was the prettiest of the bunch.

They get out of condition

Jack   You're out exercising your dog I see.

Eric	Yes, dogs have to be exercised daily, otherwise **they get out of condition.**
Jack	What's his name?
Eric	Rover.
Jack	That's a good name for a dog. Why is he woofing and wagging his tail?
Eric	Can't you see? He wants one of us to throw that stick as far as we can for him to fetch.
Jack	I can't disappoint him. Come on boys, (*throws stick*) go fetch!

He's got a taste for exotic pets

Anuj	I'm always a bit apprehensive about visiting Peter.
Urmi	Why's that? He's such a nice chap.
Anuj	He is, but **he's got a taste for exotic pets.**
Urmi	I didn't know that, such as?
Anuj	Well, last week when I was there he had a baby iguana running around the place.
Urmi	A lizard! Ugh, that would give me the creeps.
Anuj	It's not my idea of a pet. But that's not the only thing he's got. He's had a three-foot python for quite a while now as well.
Urmi	He ought to get a job in a zoo.

To be neutered

Mona	Can I see the new kittens?
Rita	Of course, they're over here with their mother in this basket.
Mona	There are five! Aren't they tiny and so sweet?
Rita	Yes, they're only a few hours old and their eyes haven't opened yet.

Mona	Is this the mother cat's first litter?
Rita	Yes it is, and happily they all seem to be healthy.
Mona	Do you expect her to have more in the future?
Rita	No, we'll be taking her to the vet **to be neutered** as soon as she has recovered from the birth.

That's my aim

Danny	I've just had a great piece of luck.
Fred	Don't tell me you've won the lottery this week.
Danny	Not quite. I've got a free weekly riding lesson at the local riding stables.
Fred	I know you love horses. How did you manage that?
Danny	I offered to muck out the stables and to help groom the horses for four hours every week.
Fred	That's not a bad bargain. It won't be long before you're an accomplished horseman if you can keep the arrangement going for any length of time.
Danny	**That's my aim.**

We must keep him on a leash

Megha	I'm really enjoying this walk in the country and so is the dog.
Sanjay	Yes, he's running here, there and everywhere.
Megha	Oh look, there are sheep in the next field!
Sanjay	I'll grab him straight away and put him on the leash. Here boy!
Megha	Thank goodness you managed to catch him before he spotted the sheep and started chasing them.
Sanjay	Yes, **we must keep him on leash** from now on. Farmers around here are likely to shoot on sight any dogs they catch worrying their sheep.

That was for the best

Lalit	The parents of children in our street are a lot less worried these days.
Rahul	Why's so?
Lalit	One of the neighbours had a very fierce dog which scared everyone. Last week it bit one of the children so badly, she had to be treated in hospital.
Rahul	That must have been an awful experience for the little girl. But why did you say they are not worried now?
Lalit	Well they complained about the dog to the police and the police forced the owner to put it down.
Rahul	Oh I see. Well I'm sure **that was for the best.**

We had to have our cat put to sleep

Rachna	What's the matter, you look as if you've been crying?
Betsy	I have, I've just come from the vet's.
Rachna	What happened?
Betsy	**We had to have our cat put to sleep.** She had a tumor which was incurable.
Rachna	Oh dear! I'm really sorry to hear that. How old was she?
Betsy	She was 15, which is quite old for a cat. But she really was like one of the family. That's why we're all so upset.

Heel girl, heel! Sit

Jaspal	Is that your new dog? What is it?
Sid	Yes, she's a chow chow and only six months old.
Jaspal	Are you taking her for a walk?
Sid	That too, but I'm also giving her obedience training.

Jaspal	Let's have a demonstration.
Sid	All right, here we go. [To the dog] **Heel girl, heel! Sit** There's a good girl.
Jaspal	That's very impressive. She came to heel and sat straight away.
Sid	Yes, she's a very obedient dog.

It's very attached to him

Sandeep	I'm sorry that the parrot is squawking its head off.
Deepak	What's the matter with it?
Sandeep	Well it's just spotted a cat outside the window and it really doesn't like cats.
Deepak	Do you ever let it out of its cage?
Sandeep	My father does. **It's very attached to him.** It perches on his shoulder and behaves itself when he's around.
Deepak	Would you ever let it out?
Sandeep	Oh no, because it's more than likely to give me a nasty nip if I do.

Kittens are always playful

Sam	Look at your brother playing with the kitten.
Radhika	Yes, he really enjoys teasing her with that piece of string.
Sam	He's holding it up so she has to jump for it.
Radhika	**Kittens are always playful,** aren't they?
Sam	Yes they are, that's why they're such fun.
Radhika	It's a pity they seem to lose much of their playfulness when they get older.

It's a cross

| Mohit | Have you seen Peter's new dog? |

Radhika	Yes I have but couldn't recognise the breed.
Mohit	That's not surprising because it's not a thoroughbred, it's a mongrel.
Radhika	Ah, that explains it. What kind of a mixture is it?
Mohit	I think **it's a cross** between a collie and a retriever.
Radhika	If that's the case it should be a very good-natured dog.

You look really chic

Gargi	Where are you off to?
Ali	I'm going to a civic reception at the town hall.
Gargi	Who's it for?
Ali	It's for a delegation from our sister city in Germany.
Gargi	Well I must say that outfit really suits you. **You look really chic.**
Ali	Thank you. I want to look my best for the foreign guests.

You've done a fantastic job

Dhruv	I've just been reading through your last project report.
Raghu	I hope you didn't find too much wrong with it.
Dhruv	On the contrary, **you've done a fantastic job.**
Raghu	Well I'm not sure about that.
Dhruv	You're too modest. It's really well organised and written and offers some very well thought out conclusions.
Raghu	Well I'm glad you like it and hope it proves useful.

Everything went like clockwork

Naina	I've just popped in to thank you very much for

organizing last weekend's trip to the seaside for the old folk.

Priyanka	That's very kind of you. They all seemed to enjoy it.
Naina	They certainly did. **Everything went like clockwork**, in fact I don't think you could have done it better.
Priyanka	I'm not sure about that, there were one or two things that could have been improved.
Naina	In a perfect world perhaps, but as far as I'm concerned it was a great success. So thank you again.

You've excelled yourself

Al	That was an absolutely delicious meal.
Isabel	I'm glad you enjoyed it. It's a recipe I haven't tried before.
Al	Your cooking is always superb but this time **you've excelled yourself.**
Isabel	Sounds like you want to get something out of me.
Al	Don't be suspicious, I really meant it.
Isabel	Well they always say that the way to a man's heart is through his stomach.

You could do just as well

Hemant	Those watercolours are really beautiful.
Gitika	I'm glad you like them. I painted them last year.
Hemant	You painted them yourself? I can't believe it, they're so good.
Gitika	They're not that good, but I'm glad you like them.
Hemant	You're so talented, I wish I had your skill.
Gitika	You should try your hand yourself, I'm sure **you could do just as well** if not better.

You have such good taste

Tanya	So this is your new apartment.
Priya	Yes, I moved in a month ago.
Tanya	Well, I have to say it looks fantastic. Did you decorate and furnish it yourself.
Priya	Yes, I did. It took me quite a lot of time.
Tanya	Well, I must say **you have such good taste** in interior decor. It could have been done by a professional designer.
Priya	Oh! I don't think so, but I'm glad you think it's nice.

I can't praise the quality of your advice too highly

John	Did you get the result you were hoping for?
Vina	Yes we did, and largely thanks to you.
John	What do you mean?
Vina	Well, it was largely your guidance that made it possible.
John	Well, I'm sure that wasn't the most important thing.
Vina	Yes, it was, and **I can't praise the quality of your advice too highly.**

The dish is too hot

Rita	I'd like to order the special please.
Waiter	I'm sorry you can't do that. **The dish is too hot.**
Rita	Please don't tell me what I can or cannot eat. I love spicy food. I can eat it so bring me the special no matter how hot it is.
Waiter	It's not spicy, I meant it's a hot item tonight and we've sold out. The special is unavailable
Rita	Ah, sorry.

You don't look a day over forty

Julie	So you're Mary's friend. I'm very pleased to meet you.
Kiran	It's a pleasure to meet you too. Mary has told me that you also working in marketing.
Julie	Yes, but as you know, she is in shoes, while I'm in cosmetics.
Kiran	Were you at school together with her?
Julie	No, no, I'm ten years older. We met much later.
Kiran	What! I can't believe it. **You don't look a day over forty.**

Your work is absolutely first-class

Gaurav	Do come in and sit down. How are you?
Hena	I'm fine, thanks. Have you had a chance to look at my proposal?
Gaurav	Yes, I have, that's what I mainly want to talk about.
Hena	I wasn't sure whether it was exactly the kind of thing you wanted.
Gaurav	Oh, have no worries. It's precisely what we need and **your work is absolutely first-class.**
Hena	Well, I must say that's a great relief.

You're head and shoulders above the others

Phagun	That's the fifth race in a row that you've won. You're by far our best driver.
Radhika	Well, I think my results are a bit flattering because I've had quite a lot of luck and our car is always so reliable.
Phagun	Nonsense, **you're head and shoulders above the others** in your division.

Radhika	Do you really think so?
Phagun	Absolutely. So much so that we are thinking of entering you in the next division for the new season.
Radhika	That means a more powerful car and longer races. It'll be a lot tougher.

You're the tops

Uma	I'm so fed up with being stuck in the house all day.
Bhawna	Well you can't expect to be up and about so soon after breaking your leg.
Uma	I suppose not, but it is very frustrating. I can't wait to get the plaster off.
Bhawna	I know, I know, but I've brought something to cheer you up.
Uma	What is it? Don't keep me in suspense.
Bhawna	It's a bottle of the very latest French perfume.
Uma	Oh, how thoughtful of you. Bhawna, **you're the tops!**

A good cause

Tanu	How many kilometers did you run?
Sapna	I ran the full course, which is just over 40 kilometers.
Tanu	And how much money did you raise for our charity?
Sapna	Almost Rs. 50,000. People were very encouraging and generous.
Tanu	Well, we'd all like to congratulate you on your achievement.
Sapna	I'm just glad to be able to contribute to **a good cause.**

For a time we thought...

Julie	Has everything been dealt with now?

Raghu	Yes, the casualties have all been taken to hospital, the electricity supply has been restored and traffic is now flowing normally.
Julie	What a difference from the chaos and confusion of two hours ago.
Raghu	Yes, **for a time we thought** we might have to call for reinforcements, but thank goodness in the end we didn't' have to.
Julie	Well it just remains for me to express our admiration for the exemplary way in which you dealt with a difficult and dangerous situation.
Raghu	I was just doing my job and I'm very glad that there were no fatalities.

I want to see the credits

Viva	Come on, let's go, the movie's over.
Sheeba	No, wait, **I want to see the credits** right through to the end.
Viva	Why, they list everybody including the studio cleaner. It'll take forever.
Sheeba	My sister's in the movie business and she worked on this movie.
Viva	Really, what does she do?
Sheeba	She's a make-up artist. Look, there she is, that's her name just coming up now. My mother will be so pleased when I tell her.

She sounds really star-struck

Jatin	My teenage sister really gets on my nerves at times.
Bakul	Why's that? Does she spend hours making up in the bathroom?

Jatin	No, it's not that, she just keeps going on and on about how wonderful Shahrukh Khan is.
Bakul	Well, a lot of girls really go for him.
Jatin	But she's got dozens of his picture all over her bedroom wall and she watches his movies over and over again on her DVD player.
Bakul	**She sounds really star-struck.**
Jatin	That's putting it mildly.

They were all dubbed into German

Simon	I've just come back from a great week in Germany, staying with my friend, but there was one thing I didn't like much.
Martin	Don't tell me it was the food?
Simon	No, of course not; that was great. It was when they showed English-language movies on TV. **They were all dubbed into German**, which rather spoiled them for me.
Martin	Your German's very good, so what was the problem?
Simon	It just seemed a bit unnatural to see Tom Hanks in an American scene with German coming out of his mouth.
Martin	But that's done for the Germans' benefit, not yours.

■ ■ ■